Social Studies & Science
Quiz Whiz
3–5

360 Quiz Questions and Answers
for Research and Review of
Social Studies and Science Concepts

Written by Linda Schwartz

Illustrated by Bev Armstrong

The Learning Works

**The
Learning
Works**

Illustrations: Bev Armstrong
Editor: Pam VanBlaricum
Text Design: Eric Larson, Studio E Books
Cover Illustration: Rick Grayson
Cover Designer: Barbara Peterson
Art Director: Tom Cochrane
Project Director: Linda Schwartz

CONTENTS

The question cards in *Social Studies & Science Quiz Whiz 3–5* are grouped into 10 categories of 36 question cards each. In each section you will find 6 folios, each with 6 cards. The 10 categories can be identified by their borders, as shown below. Levels of difficulty (I–III) can be found in the copyright footer on the answer side of each card.

Social Studies and Science Content Standards _____

The concepts presented in *Social Studies & Science Quiz Whiz 3–5* are ideal for preparing your students for standardized tests. Here are some of the content standards covered in *Social Studies & Science Quiz Whiz 3–5*:

- understand the basic structure of the U.S. government

- understand physical geography

- understand political geography

- understand the roles of famous people and places in history

- understand that plants and animals have structures for respiration, digestion, waste disposal, and transport of materials

- understand the basic operations of the human body such as blood circulation and digestion and the roles of the organs such as the heart, lungs, and stomach

- understand basic earth science such as weather and weather patterns, the solar system, and the water cycle

Ways to Use
Social Studies & Science Quiz Whiz 3–5

There are numerous ways to use *Social Studies & Science Quiz Whiz 3–5* in class. Initially, you can open the book to any page and ask a few questions to start your morning, to begin each lesson, or to fill those last minutes before lunch, recess, or the end of the day. The questions can also be assigned as research topics to get students using the Internet, the library, and reference materials in your classroom. If you wish, you can allow students to use maps for the *Quiz Whiz* geography questions.

When you have more time, here are other creative ideas:

Quiz Whiz Game

Start by removing the pages from the book and cutting the question cards apart. If you prefer to keep the book intact, simply photocopy the question cards from the section or sections you wish to use. For added durability, laminate the pages before you cut the cards apart. Different borders have been used to help you easily identify the ten sections.

Make a bulletin board display using the reproducible headers provided on pages 7 and 8. Divide each header with colored yarn. Select five categories at a time (or more if you prefer) and pin five question cards from each of the categories under each heading. Attach an unlined index card with a dollar value written on it over each question card. The most difficult questions should be worth more money and should be placed further down on the quiz board.

Once the quiz board is set up, it can be used over and over by simply changing the topics and header cards and replacing question cards with new ones. Students can get together and decide on the game rules as a class. Encourage them to add their own question cards to the classroom board. A moderator can be selected and someone can be assigned to check to see if a question has been answered correctly by simply looking on the reverse side of the question card on the board.

Select a scorekeeper to keep track of money earned. You can also use play money as *Quiz Whiz* bucks to award players. Play money can be found at many school supply and toy stores.

Tic-Tac -Toe

This is a great game to place at a social studies or science center for students to play when they've completed their class assignments. Students play with a partner taking turns picking questions from the pile and answering them. If the answer is correct, the player marks an X or an O in pencil on a Tic-Tac-Toe grid. Students must play defensively, trying to block their opponents from getting three correct answers in a row while attempting to score Tic-Tac-Toe themselves.

Quiz Whiz Bee

Use these questions for a *Quiz Whiz* Bee organized similar to a spelling bee. Students are eliminated as they miss questions asked by the teacher. Have class champs challenge each other or organize a school-wide *Quiz Whiz* Bee.

Radio or Television Game Show

Use the *Quiz Whiz* questions to organize and plan a classroom quiz show that follows a radio or television format. All the work of finding suitable questions has been done for you. Ask students to create an original quiz game that can be played as a weekly treat. Find class champs and have them compete against champs from other classes.

Quiz Whiz Question of the Day

Select one of the questions and use it as a classroom assignment each day. Students can work alone or with a partner to find the answer. Award play money to the first student or team who finds the correct answer. Play money can be found at many school supply and toy stores. The play money can be redeemed for awards at the end of the week. Another variation is to select a question each day for homework or for an extra credit challenge.

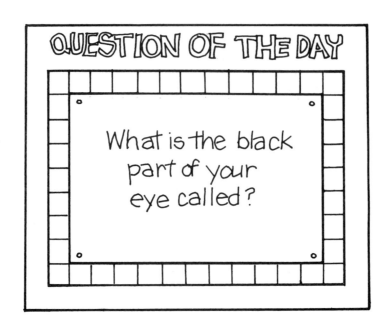

Famous People

Places & Landmarks

History & Government

Geography

Vocabulary

Plants

Mammals

Birds, Bugs, & Reptiles

The Human Body

Science Grab Bag

-» SOCIAL STUDIES & SCIENCE QUIZ WHIZ «-

Famous People

Who was the first president of the United States?

-» SOCIAL STUDIES & SCIENCE QUIZ WHIZ «-

Famous People

Which Italian explorer discovered America in 1492?

-» SOCIAL STUDIES & SCIENCE QUIZ WHIZ «-

Famous People

Who gave a famous speech that contained the words, "I have a dream"?

-» SOCIAL STUDIES & SCIENCE QUIZ WHIZ «-

Famous People

Who became president of the United States after Bill Clinton?

-» SOCIAL STUDIES & SCIENCE QUIZ WHIZ «-

Famous People

What was Orville and Wilbur's last name—the brothers who flew the first successful airplane?

-» SOCIAL STUDIES & SCIENCE QUIZ WHIZ «-

Famous People

What woman is believed to have made the first American flag?

⊷≫ SOCIAL STUDIES & SCIENCE QUIZ WHIZ ≪⊷
Famous People

Christopher Columbus

Soc. Stud. & Sci. Quiz Whiz 3–5 • Level I • Copyright © 2004 The Learning Works, Inc.

⊷≫ SOCIAL STUDIES & SCIENCE QUIZ WHIZ ≪⊷
Famous People

George Washington

Soc. Stud. & Sci. Quiz Whiz 3–5 • Level I • Copyright © 2004 The Learning Works, Inc.

⊷≫ SOCIAL STUDIES & SCIENCE QUIZ WHIZ ≪⊷
Famous People

George W. Bush

Soc. Stud. & Sci. Quiz Whiz 3–5 • Level I • Copyright © 2004 The Learning Works, Inc.

⊷≫ SOCIAL STUDIES & SCIENCE QUIZ WHIZ ≪⊷
Famous People

Martin Luther King, Jr.

Soc. Stud. & Sci. Quiz Whiz 3–5 • Level I • Copyright © 2004 The Learning Works, Inc.

⊷≫ SOCIAL STUDIES & SCIENCE QUIZ WHIZ ≪⊷
Famous People

Betsy Ross

Soc. Stud. & Sci. Quiz Whiz 3–5 • Level I • Copyright © 2004 The Learning Works, Inc.

⊷≫ SOCIAL STUDIES & SCIENCE QUIZ WHIZ ≪⊷
Famous People

Wright

Soc. Stud. & Sci. Quiz Whiz 3–5 • Level I • Copyright © 2004 The Learning Works, Inc.

-» SOCIAL STUDIES & SCIENCE QUIZ WHIZ «-
Famous People

What United States president delivered the Gettysburg Address?

-» SOCIAL STUDIES & SCIENCE QUIZ WHIZ «-
Famous People

Who was the American Indian woman who helped Captain John Smith?

-» SOCIAL STUDIES & SCIENCE QUIZ WHIZ «-
Famous People

Which president was assassinated by Lee Harvey Oswald in Dallas, Texas?

-» SOCIAL STUDIES & SCIENCE QUIZ WHIZ «-
Famous People

Who invented the telegraph: Thomas Edison, Samuel Morse, Alexander Bell, or Henry Ford?

-» SOCIAL STUDIES & SCIENCE QUIZ WHIZ «-
Famous People

Who was the queen of Spain who helped Christopher Columbus?

-» SOCIAL STUDIES & SCIENCE QUIZ WHIZ «-
Famous People

Who invented the telephone?

-» SOCIAL STUDIES & SCIENCE QUIZ WHIZ «-
Famous People

Pocahontas

-» SOCIAL STUDIES & SCIENCE QUIZ WHIZ «-
Famous People

Abraham Lincoln

-» SOCIAL STUDIES & SCIENCE QUIZ WHIZ «-
Famous People

Samuel Morse

-» SOCIAL STUDIES & SCIENCE QUIZ WHIZ «-
Famous People

John F. Kennedy

-» SOCIAL STUDIES & SCIENCE QUIZ WHIZ «-
Famous People

Alexander Graham Bell

-» SOCIAL STUDIES & SCIENCE QUIZ WHIZ «-
Famous People

Queen Isabella

Famous People

Whose picture is on the one-dollar bill?

Famous People

Who said, "Give me liberty or give me death"?

Famous People

What famous hero of the American Revolution warned the colonists that the British were coming?

Famous People

Who invented the steamboat: Alexander Fleming, Robert Fulton, Peter Cooper, or Elias Howe?

Famous People

Who served as vice president under George W. Bush?

Famous People

Who was the founder of the American Red Cross?

-» SOCIAL STUDIES & SCIENCE QUIZ WHIZ «-
Famous People

Patrick Henry

-» SOCIAL STUDIES & SCIENCE QUIZ WHIZ «-
Famous People

George Washington's

-» SOCIAL STUDIES & SCIENCE QUIZ WHIZ «-
Famous People

Robert Fulton

-» SOCIAL STUDIES & SCIENCE QUIZ WHIZ «-
Famous People

Paul Revere

-» SOCIAL STUDIES & SCIENCE QUIZ WHIZ «-
Famous People

Clara Barton

-» SOCIAL STUDIES & SCIENCE QUIZ WHIZ «-
Famous People

Richard (Dick) Cheney

-» SOCIAL STUDIES & SCIENCE QUIZ WHIZ «-

Famous People

Who was the first American woman to travel in space?

-» SOCIAL STUDIES & SCIENCE QUIZ WHIZ «-

Famous People

Who invented the cotton gin: Eli Whitney, George Pullman, Linus Yale, or Samuel Colt?

-» SOCIAL STUDIES & SCIENCE QUIZ WHIZ «-

Famous People

Who was the only United States president elected to four consecutive terms?

-» SOCIAL STUDIES & SCIENCE QUIZ WHIZ «-

Famous People

What famous American was a printer, scientist, inventor, civil servant, diplomat, and author of *Poor Richard's Almanack*?

-» SOCIAL STUDIES & SCIENCE QUIZ WHIZ «-

Famous People

Who became president after Richard Nixon resigned: Gerald Ford, Jimmy Carter, Bill Clinton, or George H.W. Bush?

-» SOCIAL STUDIES & SCIENCE QUIZ WHIZ «-

Famous People

What African-American woman is known for having refused to give up her seat on a bus in Alabama?

-» SOCIAL STUDIES & SCIENCE QUIZ WHIZ «-

Famous People

Eli Whitney

-» SOCIAL STUDIES & SCIENCE QUIZ WHIZ «-

Famous People

Sally Ride

-» SOCIAL STUDIES & SCIENCE QUIZ WHIZ «-

Famous People

Benjamin Franklin

-» SOCIAL STUDIES & SCIENCE QUIZ WHIZ «-

Famous People

Franklin Roosevelt

-» SOCIAL STUDIES & SCIENCE QUIZ WHIZ «-

Famous People

Rosa Parks

-» SOCIAL STUDIES & SCIENCE QUIZ WHIZ «-

Famous People

Gerald Ford

-» SOCIAL STUDIES & SCIENCE QUIZ WHIZ «-
Famous People

Who was the main author of the Declaration of Independence?

-» SOCIAL STUDIES & SCIENCE QUIZ WHIZ «-
Famous People

Who was the first person to fly solo nonstop across the Atlantic Ocean?

-» SOCIAL STUDIES & SCIENCE QUIZ WHIZ «-
Famous People

Who was president of the Confederate States of America?

-» SOCIAL STUDIES & SCIENCE QUIZ WHIZ «-
Famous People

Who was the first postmaster general of the United States?

-» SOCIAL STUDIES & SCIENCE QUIZ WHIZ «-
Famous People

Who said, "I only regret that I have but one life to lose for my country"?

-» SOCIAL STUDIES & SCIENCE QUIZ WHIZ «-
Famous People

Who was the first woman appointed to the U.S. Supreme Court?

-» SOCIAL STUDIES & SCIENCE QUIZ WHIZ «-
Famous People

Charles Lindbergh

-» SOCIAL STUDIES & SCIENCE QUIZ WHIZ «-
Famous People

Thomas Jefferson

-» SOCIAL STUDIES & SCIENCE QUIZ WHIZ «-
Famous People

Benjamin Franklin

-» SOCIAL STUDIES & SCIENCE QUIZ WHIZ «-
Famous People

Jefferson Davis

-» SOCIAL STUDIES & SCIENCE QUIZ WHIZ «-
Famous People

Sandra Day O'Connor

-» SOCIAL STUDIES & SCIENCE QUIZ WHIZ «-
Famous People

Nathan Hale

-» SOCIAL STUDIES & SCIENCE QUIZ WHIZ «-
Famous People

Who said, "That's one small step for man, one giant leap for mankind"?

-» SOCIAL STUDIES & SCIENCE QUIZ WHIZ «-
Famous People

Which Spanish explorer discovered Florida while looking for the fountain of youth?

-» SOCIAL STUDIES & SCIENCE QUIZ WHIZ «-
Famous People

Who was the first woman to cross the Atlantic Ocean in an airplane?

-» SOCIAL STUDIES & SCIENCE QUIZ WHIZ «-
Famous People

Who is known as the "Father of the Constitution"?

-» SOCIAL STUDIES & SCIENCE QUIZ WHIZ «-
Famous People

Who was the first president to live in the White House?

-» SOCIAL STUDIES & SCIENCE QUIZ WHIZ «-
Famous People

Who was president of the United States during most of the Civil War?

-»> SOCIAL STUDIES & SCIENCE QUIZ WHIZ «<-

Famous People

Ponce de Leon

-»> SOCIAL STUDIES & SCIENCE QUIZ WHIZ «<-

Famous People

Neil Armstrong,
the first person to
set foot on the moon

-»> SOCIAL STUDIES & SCIENCE QUIZ WHIZ «<-

Famous People

James Madison

-»> SOCIAL STUDIES & SCIENCE QUIZ WHIZ «<-

Famous People

Amelia Earhart

-»> SOCIAL STUDIES & SCIENCE QUIZ WHIZ «<-

Famous People

Abraham Lincoln

-»> SOCIAL STUDIES & SCIENCE QUIZ WHIZ «<-

Famous People

John Adams

In which state is the Empire State Building?

In what famous palace does the ruler of England live?

What does the *D.C.* stand for in Washington, D.C.?

In which state is the Alamo located?

In which country is the Great Wall located?

What southern Florida national park is home to many rare species of animals and plants?

-» SOCIAL STUDIES & SCIENCE QUIZ WHIZ «-
Places & Landmarks

Buckingham Palace

-» SOCIAL STUDIES & SCIENCE QUIZ WHIZ «-
Places & Landmarks

New York

-» SOCIAL STUDIES & SCIENCE QUIZ WHIZ «-
Places & Landmarks

Texas

-» SOCIAL STUDIES & SCIENCE QUIZ WHIZ «-
Places & Landmarks

District of Columbia

-» SOCIAL STUDIES & SCIENCE QUIZ WHIZ «-
Places & Landmarks

the Everglades

-» SOCIAL STUDIES & SCIENCE QUIZ WHIZ «-
Places & Landmarks

China

-»> SOCIAL STUDIES & SCIENCE QUIZ WHIZ «-
Places & Landmarks

What building is the official home of the president of the United States?

-»> SOCIAL STUDIES & SCIENCE QUIZ WHIZ «-
Places & Landmarks

In which state is the Gateway Arch, the tallest monument in the United States, located?

-»> SOCIAL STUDIES & SCIENCE QUIZ WHIZ «-
Places & Landmarks

What famous statue representing freedom was given to the United States by France?

-»> SOCIAL STUDIES & SCIENCE QUIZ WHIZ «-
Places & Landmarks

In which country were the first Olympic Games held?

-»> SOCIAL STUDIES & SCIENCE QUIZ WHIZ «-
Places & Landmarks

What is the capital of the United States and the headquarters of the federal government?

-»> SOCIAL STUDIES & SCIENCE QUIZ WHIZ «-
Places & Landmarks

In which state is the Golden Gate Bridge located?

Missouri

the White House

Greece

the Statue of Liberty

California

Washington, D.C.

-» SOCIAL STUDIES & SCIENCE QUIZ WHIZ «-
Places & Landmarks

What is the oldest national park in the United States?

-» SOCIAL STUDIES & SCIENCE QUIZ WHIZ «-
Places & Landmarks

In which state is the original Liberty Bell located?

-» SOCIAL STUDIES & SCIENCE QUIZ WHIZ «-
Places & Landmarks

In which country is the Wailing Wall located: Israel, Jordan, Austria, or Belgium?

-» SOCIAL STUDIES & SCIENCE QUIZ WHIZ «-
Places & Landmarks

In which state is the Great Salt Lake located?

-» SOCIAL STUDIES & SCIENCE QUIZ WHIZ «-
Places & Landmarks

Niagara Falls is located on the border between the Canadian province of Ontario and which state?

-» SOCIAL STUDIES & SCIENCE QUIZ WHIZ «-
Places & Landmarks

In which country would you find the Suez Canal: Israel, Egypt, India, or Pakistan?

-» SOCIAL STUDIES & SCIENCE QUIZ WHIZ «-
Places & Landmarks

Pennsylvania

-» SOCIAL STUDIES & SCIENCE QUIZ WHIZ «-
Places & Landmarks

Yellowstone National Park

-» SOCIAL STUDIES & SCIENCE QUIZ WHIZ «-
Places & Landmarks

Utah

-» SOCIAL STUDIES & SCIENCE QUIZ WHIZ «-
Places & Landmarks

Israel

-» SOCIAL STUDIES & SCIENCE QUIZ WHIZ «-
Places & Landmarks

Egypt

-» SOCIAL STUDIES & SCIENCE QUIZ WHIZ «-
Places & Landmarks

New York

-» SOCIAL STUDIES & SCIENCE QUIZ WHIZ «-
Places & Landmarks

What is the name of the famous steel tower located in Paris, France?

-» SOCIAL STUDIES & SCIENCE QUIZ WHIZ «-
Places & Landmarks

In which state is Mount St. Helens National Volcanic Monument located: Wyoming, Washington, Colorado, or West Virginia?

-» SOCIAL STUDIES & SCIENCE QUIZ WHIZ «-
Places & Landmarks

In which city is Independence Hall located?

-» SOCIAL STUDIES & SCIENCE QUIZ WHIZ «-
Places & Landmarks

Hollywood, California is most famous for being the center of which industry: lumber, movie, cattle, or automobile?

-» SOCIAL STUDIES & SCIENCE QUIZ WHIZ «-
Places & Landmarks

In which state is Crater Lake, the deepest lake in the United States, located: Florida, Vermont, Oregon, or Tennessee?

-» SOCIAL STUDIES & SCIENCE QUIZ WHIZ «-
Places & Landmarks

In which state is Hoover Dam, one of the world's largest hydroelectric dams, located: Missouri, Nebraska, Arkansas, or Nevada?

-»› SOCIAL STUDIES & SCIENCE QUIZ WHIZ ‹«-

Places & Landmarks

Washington

-»› SOCIAL STUDIES & SCIENCE QUIZ WHIZ ‹«-

Places & Landmarks

the Eiffel Tower

-»› SOCIAL STUDIES & SCIENCE QUIZ WHIZ ‹«-

Places & Landmarks

movie

-»› SOCIAL STUDIES & SCIENCE QUIZ WHIZ ‹«-

Places & Landmarks

Philadelphia

-»› SOCIAL STUDIES & SCIENCE QUIZ WHIZ ‹«-

Places & Landmarks

Nevada

-»› SOCIAL STUDIES & SCIENCE QUIZ WHIZ ‹«-

Places & Landmarks

Oregon

•» SOCIAL STUDIES & SCIENCE QUIZ WHIZ «•
Places & Landmarks

What is the name of the man-made canal that links the Atlantic and Pacific oceans?

•» SOCIAL STUDIES & SCIENCE QUIZ WHIZ «•
Places & Landmarks

What is the name of the international organization in New York City that helps promote world peace?

•» SOCIAL STUDIES & SCIENCE QUIZ WHIZ «•
Places & Landmarks

Which city in Italy is home to the Colosseum: Venice, Milan, Naples, or Rome?

•» SOCIAL STUDIES & SCIENCE QUIZ WHIZ «•
Places & Landmarks

In which state are the faces of four United States presidents carved into a granite cliff?

•» SOCIAL STUDIES & SCIENCE QUIZ WHIZ «•
Places & Landmarks

What is the name of the famous trail that was the main overland route to the southwestern United States before railroads?

•» SOCIAL STUDIES & SCIENCE QUIZ WHIZ «•
Places & Landmarks

In which country would you find the Taj Mahal: India, Iraq, Iran, or Indonesia?

-» SOCIAL STUDIES & SCIENCE QUIZ WHIZ «-

Places & Landmarks

the United Nations

-» SOCIAL STUDIES & SCIENCE QUIZ WHIZ «-

Places & Landmarks

the Panama Canal

-» SOCIAL STUDIES & SCIENCE QUIZ WHIZ «-

Places & Landmarks

South Dakota

-» SOCIAL STUDIES & SCIENCE QUIZ WHIZ «-

Places & Landmarks

Rome

-» SOCIAL STUDIES & SCIENCE QUIZ WHIZ «-

Places & Landmarks

India

-» SOCIAL STUDIES & SCIENCE QUIZ WHIZ «-

Places & Landmarks

the Santa Fe Trail

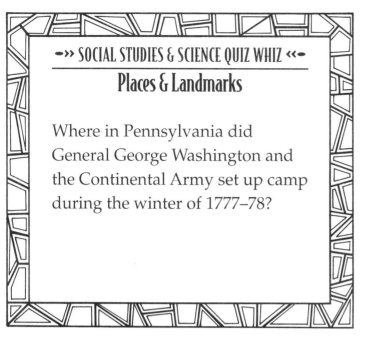

->> SOCIAL STUDIES & SCIENCE QUIZ WHIZ <<-
Places & Landmarks

Where in Pennsylvania did General George Washington and the Continental Army set up camp during the winter of 1777–78?

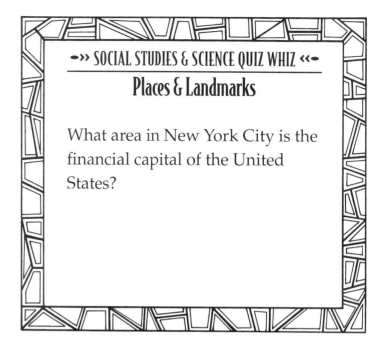

->> SOCIAL STUDIES & SCIENCE QUIZ WHIZ <<-
Places & Landmarks

What area in New York City is the financial capital of the United States?

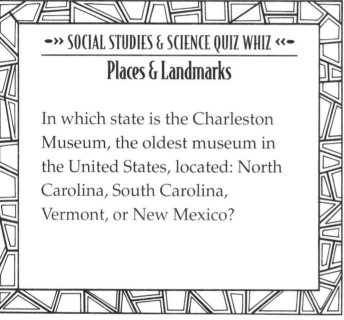

->> SOCIAL STUDIES & SCIENCE QUIZ WHIZ <<-
Places & Landmarks

In which state is the Charleston Museum, the oldest museum in the United States, located: North Carolina, South Carolina, Vermont, or New Mexico?

->> SOCIAL STUDIES & SCIENCE QUIZ WHIZ <<-
Places & Landmarks

Name the U.S. Navy base in Oahu, Hawaii, attacked by the Japanese during World War II.

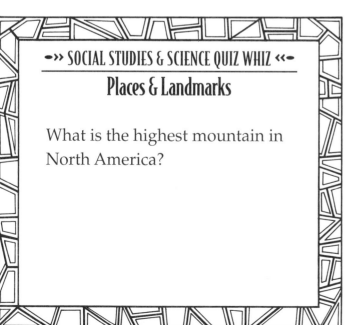

->> SOCIAL STUDIES & SCIENCE QUIZ WHIZ <<-
Places & Landmarks

What is the highest mountain in North America?

->> SOCIAL STUDIES & SCIENCE QUIZ WHIZ <<-
Places & Landmarks

In which state is Badlands National Park located: South Dakota, Alabama, Utah, or Ohio?

->» SOCIAL STUDIES & SCIENCE QUIZ WHIZ «<-
Places & Landmarks

Wall Street

->» SOCIAL STUDIES & SCIENCE QUIZ WHIZ «<-
Places & Landmarks

Valley Forge

->» SOCIAL STUDIES & SCIENCE QUIZ WHIZ «<-
Places & Landmarks

Pearl Harbor

->» SOCIAL STUDIES & SCIENCE QUIZ WHIZ «<-
Places & Landmarks

South Carolina

->» SOCIAL STUDIES & SCIENCE QUIZ WHIZ «<-
Places & Landmarks

South Dakota

->» SOCIAL STUDIES & SCIENCE QUIZ WHIZ «<-
Places & Landmarks

Mount McKinley
(Denali)

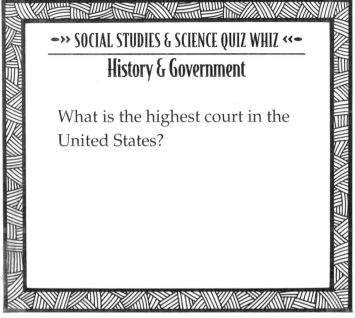

⬤≫ SOCIAL STUDIES & SCIENCE QUIZ WHIZ ≪⬤
History & Government

What is the highest court in the United States?

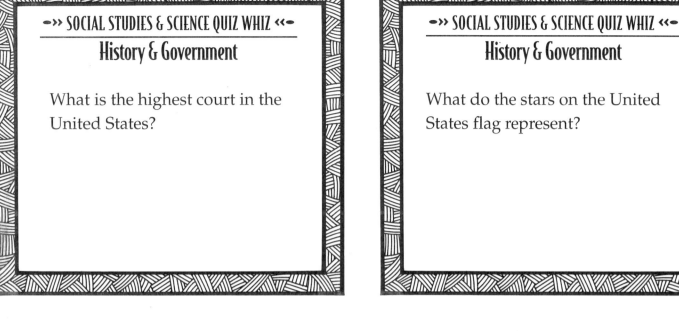

⬤≫ SOCIAL STUDIES & SCIENCE QUIZ WHIZ ≪⬤
History & Government

What do the stars on the United States flag represent?

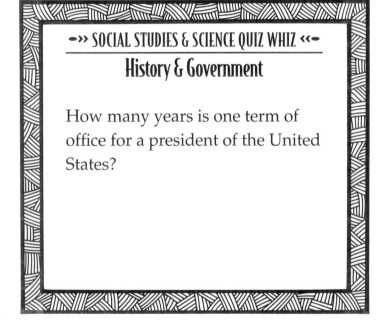

⬤≫ SOCIAL STUDIES & SCIENCE QUIZ WHIZ ≪⬤
History & Government

How many years is one term of office for a president of the United States?

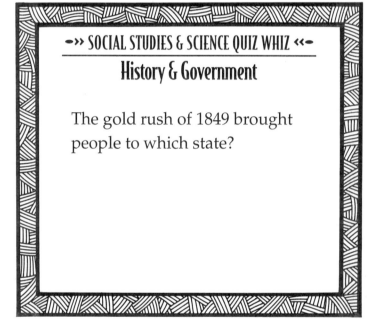

⬤≫ SOCIAL STUDIES & SCIENCE QUIZ WHIZ ≪⬤
History & Government

The gold rush of 1849 brought people to which state?

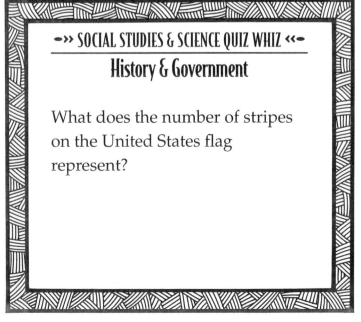

⬤≫ SOCIAL STUDIES & SCIENCE QUIZ WHIZ ≪⬤
History & Government

What does the number of stripes on the United States flag represent?

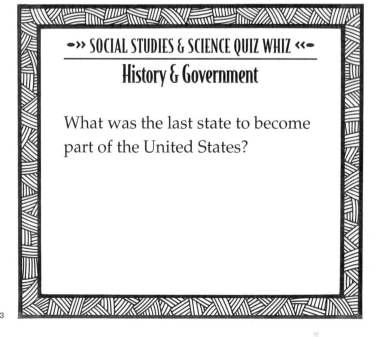

⬤≫ SOCIAL STUDIES & SCIENCE QUIZ WHIZ ≪⬤
History & Government

What was the last state to become part of the United States?

the fifty states

the Supreme Court

California

four years

Hawaii

the thirteen original colonies

-» SOCIAL STUDIES & SCIENCE QUIZ WHIZ «-
History & Government

How many people make up a jury?

-» SOCIAL STUDIES & SCIENCE QUIZ WHIZ «-
History & Government

On which ship did the Pilgrims sail to America?

-» SOCIAL STUDIES & SCIENCE QUIZ WHIZ «-
History & Government

How old must a person be to vote in national elections in the United States: 18, 21, 25, or 30?

-» SOCIAL STUDIES & SCIENCE QUIZ WHIZ «-
History & Government

How many states make up the United States of America?

-» SOCIAL STUDIES & SCIENCE QUIZ WHIZ «-
History & Government

Are places where people go to cast their votes called districts, areas, polls, or pools?

-» SOCIAL STUDIES & SCIENCE QUIZ WHIZ «-
History & Government

What were the names of the three ships in which Christopher Columbus set sail for Asia in 1492?

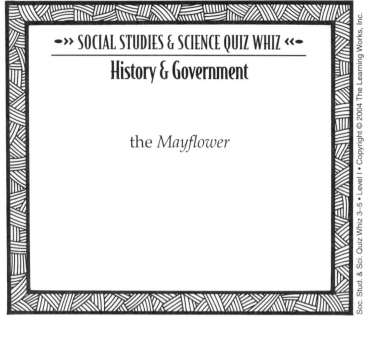

-»> SOCIAL STUDIES & SCIENCE QUIZ WHIZ «-
History & Government

the *Mayflower*

Soc. Stud. & Sci. Quiz Whiz 3–5 • Level I • Copyright © 2004 The Learning Works, Inc.

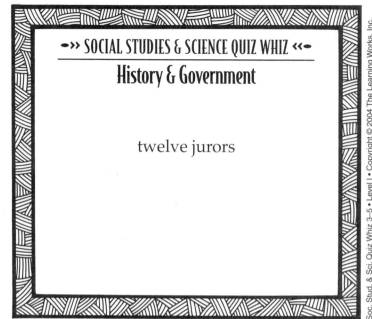

-»> SOCIAL STUDIES & SCIENCE QUIZ WHIZ «-
History & Government

twelve jurors

Soc. Stud. & Sci. Quiz Whiz 3–5 • Level I • Copyright © 2004 The Learning Works, Inc.

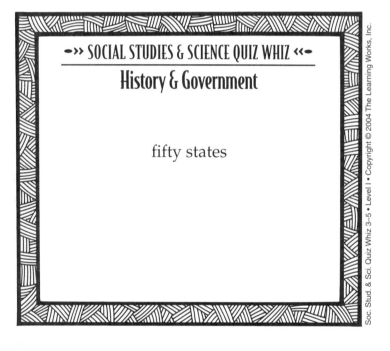

-»> SOCIAL STUDIES & SCIENCE QUIZ WHIZ «-
History & Government

fifty states

Soc. Stud. & Sci. Quiz Whiz 3–5 • Level I • Copyright © 2004 The Learning Works, Inc.

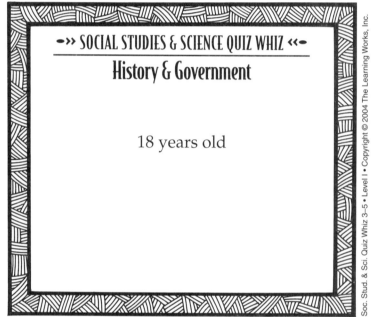

-»> SOCIAL STUDIES & SCIENCE QUIZ WHIZ «-
History & Government

18 years old

Soc. Stud. & Sci. Quiz Whiz 3–5 • Level I • Copyright © 2004 The Learning Works, Inc.

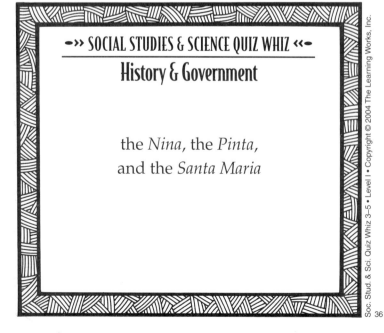

-»> SOCIAL STUDIES & SCIENCE QUIZ WHIZ «-
History & Government

the *Nina*, the *Pinta*,
and the *Santa Maria*

Soc. Stud. & Sci. Quiz Whiz 3–5 • Level I • Copyright © 2004 The Learning Works, Inc.

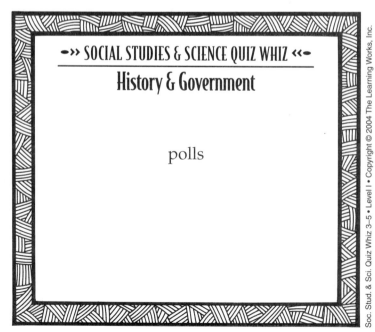

-»> SOCIAL STUDIES & SCIENCE QUIZ WHIZ «-
History & Government

polls

Soc. Stud. & Sci. Quiz Whiz 3–5 • Level I • Copyright © 2004 The Learning Works, Inc.

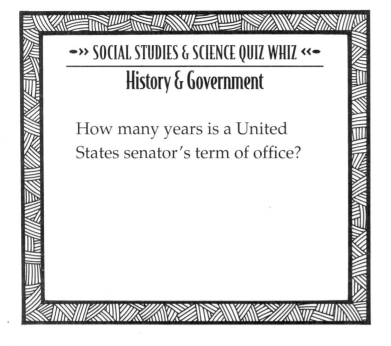

-» SOCIAL STUDIES & SCIENCE QUIZ WHIZ «-
History & Government

How many years is a United States senator's term of office?

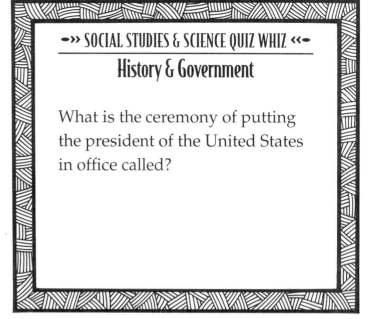

-» SOCIAL STUDIES & SCIENCE QUIZ WHIZ «-
History & Government

What is the ceremony of putting the president of the United States in office called?

-» SOCIAL STUDIES & SCIENCE QUIZ WHIZ «-
History & Government

A person must be at least how old in order to run for president of the United States?

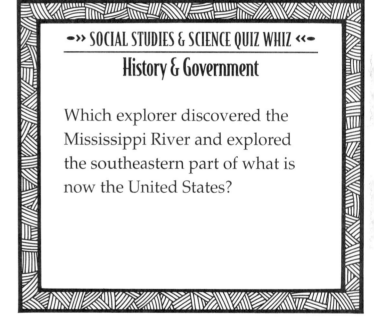

-» SOCIAL STUDIES & SCIENCE QUIZ WHIZ «-
History & Government

Which explorer discovered the Mississippi River and explored the southeastern part of what is now the United States?

-» SOCIAL STUDIES & SCIENCE QUIZ WHIZ «-
History & Government

What were the people who settled in the Plymouth Colony in Massachusetts called?

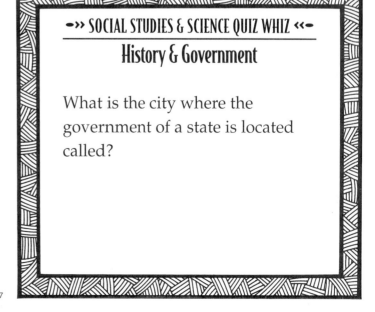

-» SOCIAL STUDIES & SCIENCE QUIZ WHIZ «-
History & Government

What is the city where the government of a state is located called?

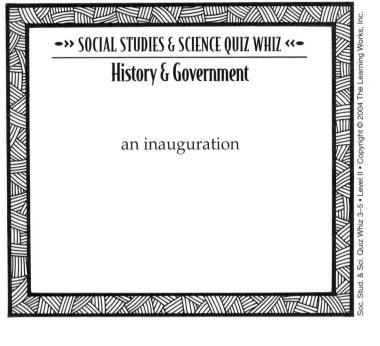

-» SOCIAL STUDIES & SCIENCE QUIZ WHIZ «-

History & Government

an inauguration

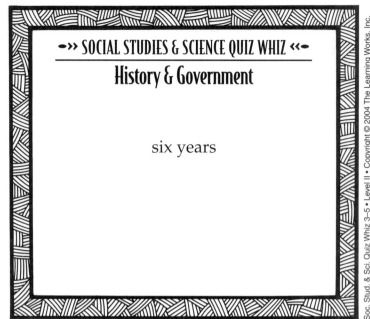

-» SOCIAL STUDIES & SCIENCE QUIZ WHIZ «-

History & Government

six years

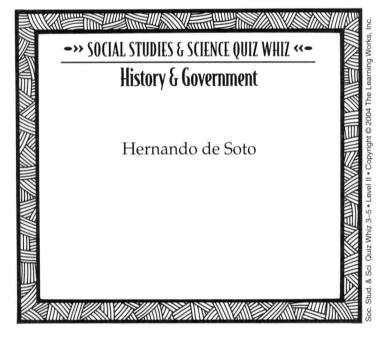

-» SOCIAL STUDIES & SCIENCE QUIZ WHIZ «-

History & Government

Hernando de Soto

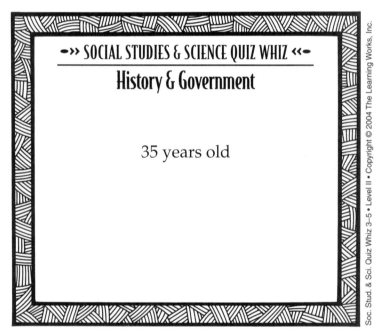

-» SOCIAL STUDIES & SCIENCE QUIZ WHIZ «-

History & Government

35 years old

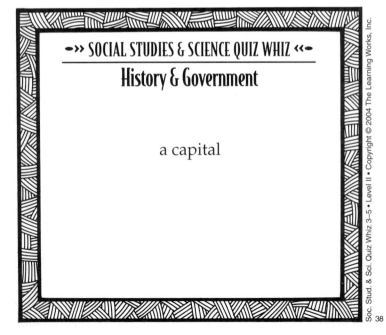

-» SOCIAL STUDIES & SCIENCE QUIZ WHIZ «-

History & Government

a capital

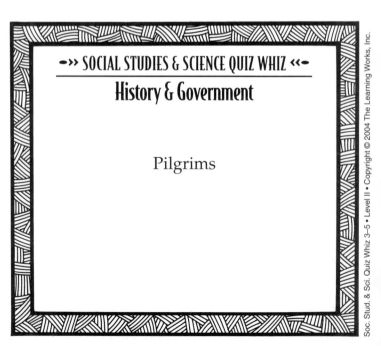

-» SOCIAL STUDIES & SCIENCE QUIZ WHIZ «-

History & Government

Pilgrims

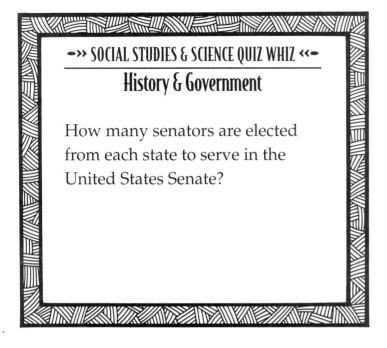

-» SOCIAL STUDIES & SCIENCE QUIZ WHIZ «-
History & Government

How many senators are elected
from each state to serve in the
United States Senate?

-» SOCIAL STUDIES & SCIENCE QUIZ WHIZ «-
History & Government

Which branch of government
makes the laws?

-» SOCIAL STUDIES & SCIENCE QUIZ WHIZ «-
History & Government

What are the names of the two
major political parties in the
United States?

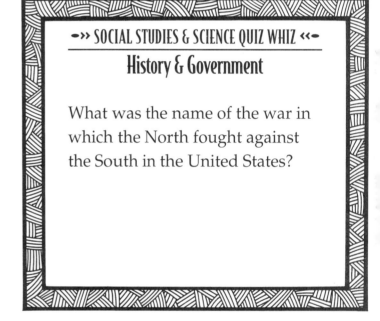

-» SOCIAL STUDIES & SCIENCE QUIZ WHIZ «-
History & Government

What was the name of the war in
which the North fought against
the South in the United States?

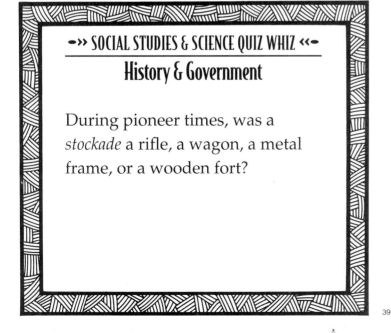

-» SOCIAL STUDIES & SCIENCE QUIZ WHIZ «-
History & Government

During pioneer times, was a
stockade a rifle, a wagon, a metal
frame, or a wooden fort?

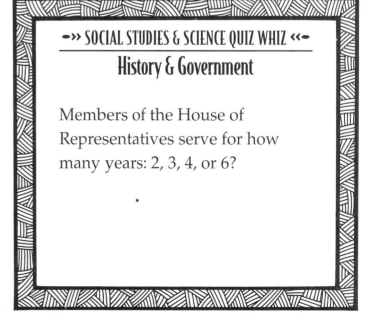

-» SOCIAL STUDIES & SCIENCE QUIZ WHIZ «-
History & Government

Members of the House of
Representatives serve for how
many years: 2, 3, 4, or 6?

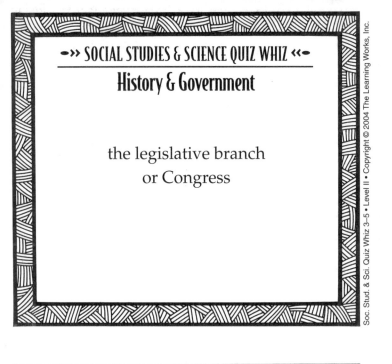

the legislative branch
or Congress

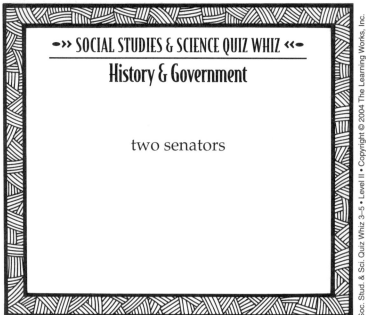

two senators

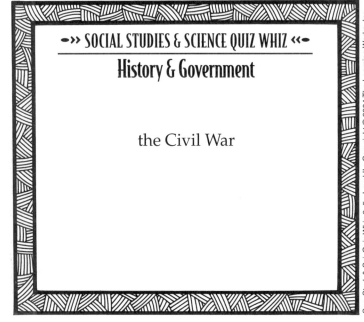

the Civil War

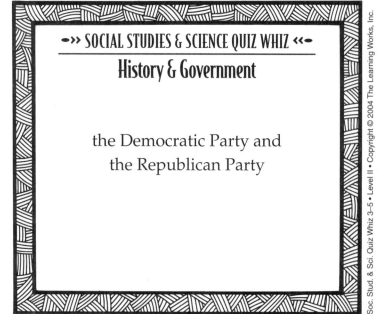

the Democratic Party and
the Republican Party

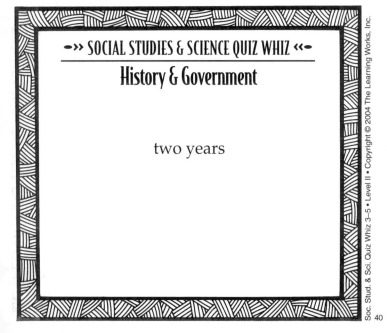

two years

a wooden fort

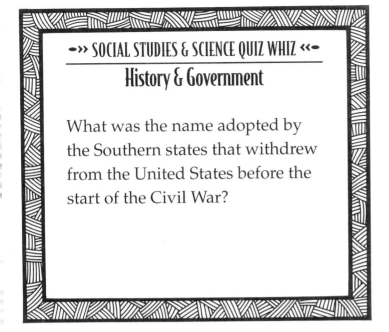

->> SOCIAL STUDIES & SCIENCE QUIZ WHIZ <<-
History & Government

What was the name adopted by the Southern states that withdrew from the United States before the start of the Civil War?

->> SOCIAL STUDIES & SCIENCE QUIZ WHIZ <<-
History & Government

How many stars were on the first flag of the United States in 1777?

->> SOCIAL STUDIES & SCIENCE QUIZ WHIZ <<-
History & Government

If there is a tie vote in the Senate, who casts the deciding vote?

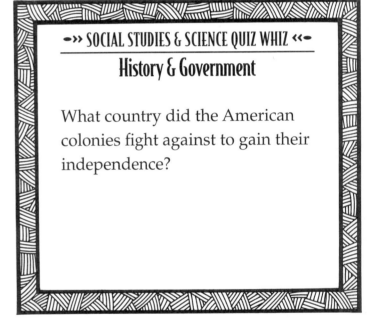

->> SOCIAL STUDIES & SCIENCE QUIZ WHIZ <<-
History & Government

What country did the American colonies fight against to gain their independence?

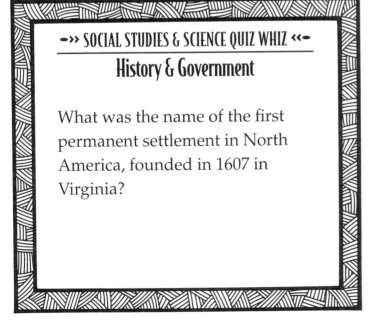

->> SOCIAL STUDIES & SCIENCE QUIZ WHIZ <<-
History & Government

What was the name of the first permanent settlement in North America, founded in 1607 in Virginia?

->> SOCIAL STUDIES & SCIENCE QUIZ WHIZ <<-
History & Government

What is a person who comes to live in a country in which he or she was not born called?

thirteen stars

the Confederacy or the Confederate States of America

Great Britain

the vice president (who is the president of the Senate)

an immigrant

Jamestown

History & Government

From which country did the United States purchase the Louisiana Territory in 1803?

History & Government

John Hancock was the first person to sign which important historical document?

History & Government

What United States document serves as "the supreme law of the land"?

History & Government

What is a person who leaves his or her own country to live in another country called?

History & Government

What country did the United States fight against in the Persian Gulf War: India, Iran, Iraq, or Greece?

History & Government

Who founded Philadelphia?

-» SOCIAL STUDIES & SCIENCE QUIZ WHIZ «-
History & Government

the Declaration of Independence

Soc. Stud. & Sci. Quiz Whiz 3–5 • Level III • Copyright © 2004 The Learning Works, Inc.

-» SOCIAL STUDIES & SCIENCE QUIZ WHIZ «-
History & Government

France

Soc. Stud. & Sci. Quiz Whiz 3–5 • Level III • Copyright © 2004 The Learning Works, Inc.

-» SOCIAL STUDIES & SCIENCE QUIZ WHIZ «-
History & Government

an emigrant

Soc. Stud. & Sci. Quiz Whiz 3–5 • Level III • Copyright © 2004 The Learning Works, Inc.

-» SOCIAL STUDIES & SCIENCE QUIZ WHIZ «-
History & Government

the United States Constitution

Soc. Stud. & Sci. Quiz Whiz 3–5 • Level III • Copyright © 2004 The Learning Works, Inc.

-» SOCIAL STUDIES & SCIENCE QUIZ WHIZ «-
History & Government

William Penn

Soc. Stud. & Sci. Quiz Whiz 3–5 • Level III • Copyright © 2004 The Learning Works, Inc.

-» SOCIAL STUDIES & SCIENCE QUIZ WHIZ «-
History & Government

Iraq

Soc. Stud. & Sci. Quiz Whiz 3–5 • Level III • Copyright © 2004 The Learning Works, Inc.

-» SOCIAL STUDIES & SCIENCE QUIZ WHIZ «-
Geography

Which ocean is the largest
in the world?

-» SOCIAL STUDIES & SCIENCE QUIZ WHIZ «-
Geography

How many continents are
there in the world?

-» SOCIAL STUDIES & SCIENCE QUIZ WHIZ «-
Geography

What is the name for a body of
land that is surrounded on all
sides by water?

-» SOCIAL STUDIES & SCIENCE QUIZ WHIZ «-
Geography

Which country borders the United
States on the south?

-» SOCIAL STUDIES & SCIENCE QUIZ WHIZ «-
Geography

On which continent is India
located?

-» SOCIAL STUDIES & SCIENCE QUIZ WHIZ «-
Geography

In what state is Death Valley
located?

Geography

seven continents

Geography

the Pacific Ocean

Geography

Mexico

Geography

an island

Geography

California

Geography

Asia

-» SOCIAL STUDIES & SCIENCE QUIZ WHIZ «-
Geography

Which country borders the United States on the north?

-» SOCIAL STUDIES & SCIENCE QUIZ WHIZ «-
Geography

On which continent is Egypt located?

-» SOCIAL STUDIES & SCIENCE QUIZ WHIZ «-
Geography

What is the name of the canyon in northwestern Arizona that is carved out of rock by the Colorado River?

-» SOCIAL STUDIES & SCIENCE QUIZ WHIZ «-
Geography

On which continent would you find the country of Peru: South America, North America, Africa, or Asia?

-» SOCIAL STUDIES & SCIENCE QUIZ WHIZ «-
Geography

What is a hot, dry, sandy area of land with few plants and little rainfall called?

-» SOCIAL STUDIES & SCIENCE QUIZ WHIZ «-
Geography

Which is not part of North America: Canada, England, the United States, or Mexico?

-»> SOCIAL STUDIES & SCIENCE QUIZ WHIZ <«-

Geography

Africa

-»> SOCIAL STUDIES & SCIENCE QUIZ WHIZ <«-

Geography

Canada

-»> SOCIAL STUDIES & SCIENCE QUIZ WHIZ <«-

Geography

South America

-»> SOCIAL STUDIES & SCIENCE QUIZ WHIZ <«-

Geography

the Grand Canyon

-»> SOCIAL STUDIES & SCIENCE QUIZ WHIZ <«-

Geography

England

-»> SOCIAL STUDIES & SCIENCE QUIZ WHIZ <«-

Geography

a desert

·» SOCIAL STUDIES & SCIENCE QUIZ WHIZ «·
Geography

Which is the largest and most northerly state in the United States?

·» SOCIAL STUDIES & SCIENCE QUIZ WHIZ «·
Geography

What is the area of land at the mouth of a river called?

·» SOCIAL STUDIES & SCIENCE QUIZ WHIZ «·
Geography

England is considered to be a part of which continent?

·» SOCIAL STUDIES & SCIENCE QUIZ WHIZ «·
Geography

What is the name of the large body of water surrounded by Mexico and the southern coast of the United States?

·» SOCIAL STUDIES & SCIENCE QUIZ WHIZ «·
Geography

Which mountain range is not found in the United States: the Sierra Nevada, the Alps, the Rocky Mountains, or the Appalachian Mountains?

·» SOCIAL STUDIES & SCIENCE QUIZ WHIZ «·
Geography

What is an area of land surrounded by water on three sides called?

⊸» SOCIAL STUDIES & SCIENCE QUIZ WHIZ «⊸
Geography

a delta

⊸» SOCIAL STUDIES & SCIENCE QUIZ WHIZ «⊸
Geography

Alaska

⊸» SOCIAL STUDIES & SCIENCE QUIZ WHIZ «⊸
Geography

the Gulf of Mexico

⊸» SOCIAL STUDIES & SCIENCE QUIZ WHIZ «⊸
Geography

Europe

⊸» SOCIAL STUDIES & SCIENCE QUIZ WHIZ «⊸
Geography

a peninsula

⊸» SOCIAL STUDIES & SCIENCE QUIZ WHIZ «⊸
Geography

the Alps

-» SOCIAL STUDIES & SCIENCE QUIZ WHIZ «-
Geography

What is the longest river in the world?

-» SOCIAL STUDIES & SCIENCE QUIZ WHIZ «-
Geography

Is Mississippi north, south, east, or west of Alabama?

-» SOCIAL STUDIES & SCIENCE QUIZ WHIZ «-
Geography

Which country in Europe is shaped like a boot?

-» SOCIAL STUDIES & SCIENCE QUIZ WHIZ «-
Geography

What is a natural stream of water falling from a high place called?

-» SOCIAL STUDIES & SCIENCE QUIZ WHIZ «-
Geography

What is the largest island in the world?

-» SOCIAL STUDIES & SCIENCE QUIZ WHIZ «-
Geography

Is California north, south, east, or west of Oregon?

-» SOCIAL STUDIES & SCIENCE QUIZ WHIZ «-

Geography

west

-» SOCIAL STUDIES & SCIENCE QUIZ WHIZ «-

Geography

the Nile River

-» SOCIAL STUDIES & SCIENCE QUIZ WHIZ «-

Geography

a waterfall

-» SOCIAL STUDIES & SCIENCE QUIZ WHIZ «-

Geography

Italy

-» SOCIAL STUDIES & SCIENCE QUIZ WHIZ «-

Geography

south

-» SOCIAL STUDIES & SCIENCE QUIZ WHIZ «-

Geography

Greenland

-» SOCIAL STUDIES & SCIENCE QUIZ WHIZ «-
Geography

Which Canadian city is known as "Canada's Gateway to the Pacific" and is the largest city in the province of British Columbia?

-» SOCIAL STUDIES & SCIENCE QUIZ WHIZ «-
Geography

Is Kansas north, south, east, or west of Colorado?

-» SOCIAL STUDIES & SCIENCE QUIZ WHIZ «-
Geography

Which of the following states is directly north of Wyoming: Colorado, Montana, Nebraska, or Idaho?

-» SOCIAL STUDIES & SCIENCE QUIZ WHIZ «-
Geography

What is a river or stream that flows into a larger river called?

-» SOCIAL STUDIES & SCIENCE QUIZ WHIZ «-
Geography

Is Georgia north, south, east, or west of Florida?

-» SOCIAL STUDIES & SCIENCE QUIZ WHIZ «-
Geography

Which state is directly north of Oklahoma?

-» SOCIAL STUDIES & SCIENCE QUIZ WHIZ «-

Geography

east

Soc. Stud. & Sci. Quiz Whiz 3–5 • Level III • Copyright © 2004 The Learning Works, Inc.

-» SOCIAL STUDIES & SCIENCE QUIZ WHIZ «-

Geography

Vancouver

Soc. Stud. & Sci. Quiz Whiz 3–5 • Level III • Copyright © 2004 The Learning Works, Inc.

-» SOCIAL STUDIES & SCIENCE QUIZ WHIZ «-

Geography

a tributary

Soc. Stud. & Sci. Quiz Whiz 3–5 • Level III • Copyright © 2004 The Learning Works, Inc.

-» SOCIAL STUDIES & SCIENCE QUIZ WHIZ «-

Geography

Montana

Soc. Stud. & Sci. Quiz Whiz 3–5 • Level III • Copyright © 2004 The Learning Works, Inc.

-» SOCIAL STUDIES & SCIENCE QUIZ WHIZ «-

Geography

Kansas

Soc. Stud. & Sci. Quiz Whiz 3–5 • Level III • Copyright © 2004 The Learning Works, Inc.

-» SOCIAL STUDIES & SCIENCE QUIZ WHIZ «-

Geography

north

Soc. Stud. & Sci. Quiz Whiz 3–5 • Level III • Copyright © 2004 The Learning Works, Inc.

-» SOCIAL STUDIES & SCIENCE QUIZ WHIZ «-
Geography

Which state is directly east of Tennessee?

-» SOCIAL STUDIES & SCIENCE QUIZ WHIZ «-
Geography

Is a narrow strip of land that connects two larger land areas called a bay, a reef, an isthmus, or a canyon?

-» SOCIAL STUDIES & SCIENCE QUIZ WHIZ «-
Geography

Which state is directly north of Arkansas?

-» SOCIAL STUDIES & SCIENCE QUIZ WHIZ «-
Geography

Is a hill or mountain with a flat top and steep sides called a mesa, a levee, a fjord, or a bayou?

-» SOCIAL STUDIES & SCIENCE QUIZ WHIZ «-
Geography

Is Illinois north, south, east, or west of Wisconsin?

-» SOCIAL STUDIES & SCIENCE QUIZ WHIZ «-
Geography

Which state is directly west of New Mexico?

-» SOCIAL STUDIES & SCIENCE QUIZ WHIZ «-

Geography

an isthmus

-» SOCIAL STUDIES & SCIENCE QUIZ WHIZ «-

Geography

North Carolina

-» SOCIAL STUDIES & SCIENCE QUIZ WHIZ «-

Geography

a mesa

-» SOCIAL STUDIES & SCIENCE QUIZ WHIZ «-

Geography

Missouri

-» SOCIAL STUDIES & SCIENCE QUIZ WHIZ «-

Geography

Arizona

-» SOCIAL STUDIES & SCIENCE QUIZ WHIZ «-

Geography

south

-» SOCIAL STUDIES & SCIENCE QUIZ WHIZ «-
Vocabulary

What is a sphere with a map of the world printed on it called?

-» SOCIAL STUDIES & SCIENCE QUIZ WHIZ «-
Vocabulary

Is Utah a city, a state, a country, or a continent?

-» SOCIAL STUDIES & SCIENCE QUIZ WHIZ «-
Vocabulary

Is a large urban area where many people live and work called a chamber, a clan, a circuit, or a city?

-» SOCIAL STUDIES & SCIENCE QUIZ WHIZ «-
Vocabulary

Which word means *to choose by voting*: elevate, elect, educate, or impeach?

-» SOCIAL STUDIES & SCIENCE QUIZ WHIZ «-
Vocabulary

What is a book of maps called?

-» SOCIAL STUDIES & SCIENCE QUIZ WHIZ «-
Vocabulary

What is a strong building or area that can be defended against attack called: a forum, a fort, a fossil, or a formation?

-» SOCIAL STUDIES & SCIENCE QUIZ WHIZ «-
Vocabulary

a state

-» SOCIAL STUDIES & SCIENCE QUIZ WHIZ «-
Vocabulary

a globe

-» SOCIAL STUDIES & SCIENCE QUIZ WHIZ «-
Vocabulary

elect

-» SOCIAL STUDIES & SCIENCE QUIZ WHIZ «-
Vocabulary

a city

-» SOCIAL STUDIES & SCIENCE QUIZ WHIZ «-
Vocabulary

a fort

-» SOCIAL STUDIES & SCIENCE QUIZ WHIZ «-
Vocabulary

an atlas

▪» SOCIAL STUDIES & SCIENCE QUIZ WHIZ «▪
Vocabulary

What is a large wagon with a canvas top spread over hoops called?

▪» SOCIAL STUDIES & SCIENCE QUIZ WHIZ «▪
Vocabulary

What is a time of armed fighting between countries or groups within a country called?

▪» SOCIAL STUDIES & SCIENCE QUIZ WHIZ «▪
Vocabulary

Is a person who is among the first to explore and settle a region called a pirate, a pioneer, a pilgrim, or a pilot?

▪» SOCIAL STUDIES & SCIENCE QUIZ WHIZ «▪
Vocabulary

What are underground railroads built in busy cities called?

▪» SOCIAL STUDIES & SCIENCE QUIZ WHIZ «▪
Vocabulary

If the president of the United States dies while in office, who becomes the president?

▪» SOCIAL STUDIES & SCIENCE QUIZ WHIZ «▪
Vocabulary

What is a room or building where trials are held called?

-» SOCIAL STUDIES & SCIENCE QUIZ WHIZ «-

Vocabulary

a war

-» SOCIAL STUDIES & SCIENCE QUIZ WHIZ «-

Vocabulary

a covered wagon or Conestoga wagon

-» SOCIAL STUDIES & SCIENCE QUIZ WHIZ «-

Vocabulary

subways

-» SOCIAL STUDIES & SCIENCE QUIZ WHIZ «-

Vocabulary

a pioneer

-» SOCIAL STUDIES & SCIENCE QUIZ WHIZ «-

Vocabulary

a court
(courtroom, courthouse)

-» SOCIAL STUDIES & SCIENCE QUIZ WHIZ «-

Vocabulary

the vice president

-» SOCIAL STUDIES & SCIENCE QUIZ WHIZ «-
Vocabulary

What is a member of the senate called: a senior, a select person, a senator, or a serf?

-» SOCIAL STUDIES & SCIENCE QUIZ WHIZ «-
Vocabulary

What is a system of government that is run by the people who live under it called?

-» SOCIAL STUDIES & SCIENCE QUIZ WHIZ «-
Vocabulary

Is a *hogan* the name of an Indian food, dance, weapon, or house?

-» SOCIAL STUDIES & SCIENCE QUIZ WHIZ «-
Vocabulary

What is an official count of the people living in a district or country called?

-» SOCIAL STUDIES & SCIENCE QUIZ WHIZ «-
Vocabulary

In the United States, is a person elected to be the head of government of a state called a justice, a governor, a prime minister, or a judge?

-» SOCIAL STUDIES & SCIENCE QUIZ WHIZ «-
Vocabulary

To what do "Old Glory" and the "Stars and Stripes" refer?

-» SOCIAL STUDIES & SCIENCE QUIZ WHIZ «-

Vocabulary

a democracy

-» SOCIAL STUDIES & SCIENCE QUIZ WHIZ «-

Vocabulary

a senator

-» SOCIAL STUDIES & SCIENCE QUIZ WHIZ «-

Vocabulary

a census

-» SOCIAL STUDIES & SCIENCE QUIZ WHIZ «-

Vocabulary

a house

-» SOCIAL STUDIES & SCIENCE QUIZ WHIZ «-

Vocabulary

the United States flag

-» SOCIAL STUDIES & SCIENCE QUIZ WHIZ «-

Vocabulary

a governor

-»> SOCIAL STUDIES & SCIENCE QUIZ WHIZ «-
Vocabulary

Is a person who rules a country without sharing power called a dictator, a deputy, a mayor, or a debtor?

-»> SOCIAL STUDIES & SCIENCE QUIZ WHIZ «-
Vocabulary

What is a ditch filled with water that surrounds a castle called?

-»> SOCIAL STUDIES & SCIENCE QUIZ WHIZ «-
Vocabulary

Is the land next to the sea called a sand bar, a tide, a coast, or a pier?

-»> SOCIAL STUDIES & SCIENCE QUIZ WHIZ «-
Vocabulary

What is money that people and businesses pay the government for its services and support called?

-»> SOCIAL STUDIES & SCIENCE QUIZ WHIZ «-
Vocabulary

What was the system of delivering mail by horseback between St. Joseph, Missouri, and Sacramento, California, called?

-»> SOCIAL STUDIES & SCIENCE QUIZ WHIZ «-
Vocabulary

Is the "Star-Spangled Banner," written by Francis Scott Key, called a national anthem, a musical, an opera, or an ode?

SOCIAL STUDIES & SCIENCE QUIZ WHIZ
Vocabulary

a moat

Soc. Stud. & Sci. Quiz Whiz 3–5 • Level II • Copyright © 2004 The Learning Works, Inc.

SOCIAL STUDIES & SCIENCE QUIZ WHIZ
Vocabulary

a dictator

Soc. Stud. & Sci. Quiz Whiz 3–5 • Level II • Copyright © 2004 The Learning Works, Inc.

SOCIAL STUDIES & SCIENCE QUIZ WHIZ
Vocabulary

taxes

Soc. Stud. & Sci. Quiz Whiz 3–5 • Level II • Copyright © 2004 The Learning Works, Inc.

SOCIAL STUDIES & SCIENCE QUIZ WHIZ
Vocabulary

a coast

Soc. Stud. & Sci. Quiz Whiz 3–5 • Level II • Copyright © 2004 The Learning Works, Inc.

SOCIAL STUDIES & SCIENCE QUIZ WHIZ
Vocabulary

a national anthem

Soc. Stud. & Sci. Quiz Whiz 3–5 • Level II • Copyright © 2004 The Learning Works, Inc.

SOCIAL STUDIES & SCIENCE QUIZ WHIZ
Vocabulary

the Pony Express

Soc. Stud. & Sci. Quiz Whiz 3–5 • Level II • Copyright © 2004 The Learning Works, Inc.

–» SOCIAL STUDIES & SCIENCE QUIZ WHIZ «–
Vocabulary

What do the letters FBI stand for in the United States government?

–» SOCIAL STUDIES & SCIENCE QUIZ WHIZ «–
Vocabulary

Which house of Congress is based on each state's population according to the most recent census?

–» SOCIAL STUDIES & SCIENCE QUIZ WHIZ «–
Vocabulary

What is a person who explores for gold or other minerals called?

–» SOCIAL STUDIES & SCIENCE QUIZ WHIZ «–
Vocabulary

Is the president's rejection of a bill passed by a legislature called a session, a veto, a visa, or a draft?

–» SOCIAL STUDIES & SCIENCE QUIZ WHIZ «–
Vocabulary

Are goods from another country that are brought in for sale or use called impacts, imports, immigrants, or exports?

–» SOCIAL STUDIES & SCIENCE QUIZ WHIZ «–
Vocabulary

Is a formal agreement between countries called a tribute, a treaty, a veto, or treason?

⇢» SOCIAL STUDIES & SCIENCE QUIZ WHIZ «⇠

Vocabulary

the House of Representatives

⇢» SOCIAL STUDIES & SCIENCE QUIZ WHIZ «⇠

Vocabulary

Federal Bureau of Investigation

⇢» SOCIAL STUDIES & SCIENCE QUIZ WHIZ «⇠

Vocabulary

a veto

⇢» SOCIAL STUDIES & SCIENCE QUIZ WHIZ «⇠

Vocabulary

a prospector

⇢» SOCIAL STUDIES & SCIENCE QUIZ WHIZ «⇠

Vocabulary

a treaty

⇢» SOCIAL STUDIES & SCIENCE QUIZ WHIZ «⇠

Vocabulary

imports

->» SOCIAL STUDIES & SCIENCE QUIZ WHIZ «<-
Vocabulary

What is the study of the way humans lived a long time ago called: botany, archaeology, architecture, or astronomy?

->» SOCIAL STUDIES & SCIENCE QUIZ WHIZ «<-
Vocabulary

What are the first ten amendments to the United States Constitution called?

->» SOCIAL STUDIES & SCIENCE QUIZ WHIZ «<-
Vocabulary

Is something that is sold or traded to another country called an import, a visa, a tariff, or an export?

->» SOCIAL STUDIES & SCIENCE QUIZ WHIZ «<-
Vocabulary

What is the system of overlapping the powers of the three branches of government so each can check the actions of the others called?

->» SOCIAL STUDIES & SCIENCE QUIZ WHIZ «<-
Vocabulary

Is a change in the United States Constitution called a recall, an amendment, a tariff, or a bill?

->» SOCIAL STUDIES & SCIENCE QUIZ WHIZ «<-
Vocabulary

What is the metal covering for the body that was worn for protection during battle in former times called?

Vocabulary

the Bill of Rights

Vocabulary

archaeology

Vocabulary

checks and balances

Vocabulary

an export

Vocabulary

armor

Vocabulary

an amendment

->» SOCIAL STUDIES & SCIENCE QUIZ WHIZ «<-
Plants

Which of the following is *not* a fruit: orange, pear, broccoli, or apple?

->» SOCIAL STUDIES & SCIENCE QUIZ WHIZ «<-
Plants

What part of a plant anchors it in the ground?

->» SOCIAL STUDIES & SCIENCE QUIZ WHIZ «<-
Plants

What are the sharp points on the branch or stem of a rose called?

->» SOCIAL STUDIES & SCIENCE QUIZ WHIZ «<-
Plants

What part of a flower holds the pollen: the petal, leaf, stamen, or root?

->» SOCIAL STUDIES & SCIENCE QUIZ WHIZ «<-
Plants

Do cherries grow on bushes, vines, or trees?

->» SOCIAL STUDIES & SCIENCE QUIZ WHIZ «<-
Plants

What is the name of the main stem of a tree from which branches grow?

-»› SOCIAL STUDIES & SCIENCE QUIZ WHIZ ‹«-

Plants

the roots

-»› SOCIAL STUDIES & SCIENCE QUIZ WHIZ ‹«-

Plants

broccoli

-»› SOCIAL STUDIES & SCIENCE QUIZ WHIZ ‹«-

Plants

stamen

-»› SOCIAL STUDIES & SCIENCE QUIZ WHIZ ‹«-

Plants

thorns

-»› SOCIAL STUDIES & SCIENCE QUIZ WHIZ ‹«-

Plants

the trunk

-»› SOCIAL STUDIES & SCIENCE QUIZ WHIZ ‹«-

Plants

trees

-»> SOCIAL STUDIES & SCIENCE QUIZ WHIZ «<-
Plants

When you eat a carrot, are you eating the plant's leaves, flowers, roots, or stems?

-»> SOCIAL STUDIES & SCIENCE QUIZ WHIZ «<-
Plants

What part of a plant supports the leaves and flowers and carries water and food to all parts of the plant?

-»> SOCIAL STUDIES & SCIENCE QUIZ WHIZ «<-
Plants

Do watermelons grow on vines, trees, or bushes?

-»> SOCIAL STUDIES & SCIENCE QUIZ WHIZ «<-
Plants

Which of these foods come from a plant's leaves: beets, lettuce, cucumbers, or bananas?

-»> SOCIAL STUDIES & SCIENCE QUIZ WHIZ «<-
Plants

What is the seed or nut of an oak tree called: a peanut, a cashew, an acorn, or a walnut?

-»> SOCIAL STUDIES & SCIENCE QUIZ WHIZ «<-
Plants

Which part of the plant makes seeds: the root, stem, flower, or petal?

→» SOCIAL STUDIES & SCIENCE QUIZ WHIZ «←

Plants

the stem

→» SOCIAL STUDIES & SCIENCE QUIZ WHIZ «←

Plants

roots

→» SOCIAL STUDIES & SCIENCE QUIZ WHIZ «←

Plants

lettuce

→» SOCIAL STUDIES & SCIENCE QUIZ WHIZ «←

Plants

vines

→» SOCIAL STUDIES & SCIENCE QUIZ WHIZ «←

Plants

flower

→» SOCIAL STUDIES & SCIENCE QUIZ WHIZ «←

Plants

an acorn

-» SOCIAL STUDIES & SCIENCE QUIZ WHIZ «-
Plants

What are trees that stay green throughout the year called?

-» SOCIAL STUDIES & SCIENCE QUIZ WHIZ «-
Plants

Which of the following do *not* grow in pods: peas, beans, or corn?

-» SOCIAL STUDIES & SCIENCE QUIZ WHIZ «-
Plants

Are the thin, pointed leaves on fir and pine trees called spores, needles, fronds, or buds?

-» SOCIAL STUDIES & SCIENCE QUIZ WHIZ «-
Plants

Is a cactus covered with leaves, thorns, spines, or petals?

-» SOCIAL STUDIES & SCIENCE QUIZ WHIZ «-
Plants

Which is *not* the name of a tree: cedar, spruce, kale, or redwood?

-» SOCIAL STUDIES & SCIENCE QUIZ WHIZ «-
Plants

Are fronds the leaves of ferns, daisies, tulips, or roses?

-» SOCIAL STUDIES & SCIENCE QUIZ WHIZ «-

Plants

corn

-» SOCIAL STUDIES & SCIENCE QUIZ WHIZ «-

Plants

evergreens

-» SOCIAL STUDIES & SCIENCE QUIZ WHIZ «-

Plants

spines

-» SOCIAL STUDIES & SCIENCE QUIZ WHIZ «-

Plants

needles

-» SOCIAL STUDIES & SCIENCE QUIZ WHIZ «-

Plants

ferns

-» SOCIAL STUDIES & SCIENCE QUIZ WHIZ «-

Plants

kale

⋅» SOCIAL STUDIES & SCIENCE QUIZ WHIZ «⋅
Plants

What is a plant that lives only one year or growing season called?

⋅» SOCIAL STUDIES & SCIENCE QUIZ WHIZ «⋅
Plants

Which of these flowers grow bulbs: asters, buttercups, tulips, or petunias?

⋅» SOCIAL STUDIES & SCIENCE QUIZ WHIZ «⋅
Plants

Is the part of a plant that is fleshy and holds the seeds the leaf, stem, fruit, or root?

⋅» SOCIAL STUDIES & SCIENCE QUIZ WHIZ «⋅
Plants

Which of these vegetables grows underground: cauliflower, potato, spinach, or beans?

⋅» SOCIAL STUDIES & SCIENCE QUIZ WHIZ «⋅
Plants

What is the tiny stalk in the center of a flower where seeds develop called?

⋅» SOCIAL STUDIES & SCIENCE QUIZ WHIZ «⋅
Plants

Is a mushroom a type of algae, fungus, evergreen, or annual?

-» SOCIAL STUDIES & SCIENCE QUIZ WHIZ «-
Plants

tulips

-» SOCIAL STUDIES & SCIENCE QUIZ WHIZ «-
Plants

an annual

-» SOCIAL STUDIES & SCIENCE QUIZ WHIZ «-
Plants

potato

-» SOCIAL STUDIES & SCIENCE QUIZ WHIZ «-
Plants

the fruit

-» SOCIAL STUDIES & SCIENCE QUIZ WHIZ «-
Plants

fungus

-» SOCIAL STUDIES & SCIENCE QUIZ WHIZ «-
Plants

the pistil

Plants

Which of these is *not* needed for photosynthesis to occur: water, sunlight, air, or soil?

Plants

What is a person who studies plants called?

Plants

What are green plants that don't have any roots, stems, or leaves and live in moist soil or water called?

Plants

What is a young plant that is grown from a seed called?

Plants

Which is *not* a type of grain: oats, peas, wheat, or corn?

Plants

Is a new young shoot which has been inserted into another living plant in the hope that they will grow together called a twig, a graft, a bond, or a transfer?

->» SOCIAL STUDIES & SCIENCE QUIZ WHIZ «<-
Plants

a botanist

->» SOCIAL STUDIES & SCIENCE QUIZ WHIZ «<-
Plants

soil

->» SOCIAL STUDIES & SCIENCE QUIZ WHIZ «<-
Plants

a seedling

->» SOCIAL STUDIES & SCIENCE QUIZ WHIZ «<-
Plants

algae

->» SOCIAL STUDIES & SCIENCE QUIZ WHIZ «<-
Plants

a graft

->» SOCIAL STUDIES & SCIENCE QUIZ WHIZ «<-
Plants

peas

Plants

What is the green substance in plants that absorbs energy from sunlight called?

Plants

What part of the plant makes most of the food it needs to live and grow?

Plants

Which of the following is *not* a type of flower: heather, marigold, holly, or rhododendron?

Plants

What is a plant whose roots, leaves, or other parts are used as food called: a zinnia, a vegetable, a lilac, or an iris?

Plants

What is the yellowish powder made in the anthers of flowers called?

Plants

Which of the following do *not* produce spores: firs, mushrooms, or ferns?

the leaves

chlorophyll

a vegetable

holly

firs

pollen

Mammals

Which is *not* a characteristic of a mammal: has a backbone, nurses its young, is cold-blooded, or is covered with fur or hair?

Mammals

What do you call a group of elephants?

Mammals

What is the smallest breed of dog: poodle, pug, chihuahua, or beagle?

Mammals

What term is given to the wintertime sleep of animals such as bears and woodchucks?

Mammals

Which of the following is *not* a mammal: a whale, a human being, a condor, or a koala?

Mammals

What is a baby lion called?

SOCIAL STUDIES & SCIENCE QUIZ WHIZ
Mammals

a herd

SOCIAL STUDIES & SCIENCE QUIZ WHIZ
Mammals

is cold-blooded

SOCIAL STUDIES & SCIENCE QUIZ WHIZ
Mammals

hibernation
or hibernate

SOCIAL STUDIES & SCIENCE QUIZ WHIZ
Mammals

chihuahua

SOCIAL STUDIES & SCIENCE QUIZ WHIZ
Mammals

a cub

SOCIAL STUDIES & SCIENCE QUIZ WHIZ
Mammals

condor

-» SOCIAL STUDIES & SCIENCE QUIZ WHIZ «-
Mammals

What is a baby giraffe called?

-» SOCIAL STUDIES & SCIENCE QUIZ WHIZ «-
Mammals

On which mammal would you find antlers: bears, deer, tigers, or cows?

-» SOCIAL STUDIES & SCIENCE QUIZ WHIZ «-
Mammals

What is the name of the hard, white substance that makes up the tusks of elephants and walruses?

-» SOCIAL STUDIES & SCIENCE QUIZ WHIZ «-
Mammals

Which of the following is *not* a type of horse: palomino, pinto, thoroughbred, or bison?

-» SOCIAL STUDIES & SCIENCE QUIZ WHIZ «-
Mammals

A hare is most like which of the following: rabbit, bear, rodent, or cat?

-» SOCIAL STUDIES & SCIENCE QUIZ WHIZ «-
Mammals

What plant must pandas have in order to survive?

deer

a calf

bison

ivory

bamboo

rabbit

-» SOCIAL STUDIES & SCIENCE QUIZ WHIZ «-

Mammals

What name is given to the group of animals that have spinal cords encased in backbones?

-» SOCIAL STUDIES & SCIENCE QUIZ WHIZ «-

Mammals

What is the largest and strongest land animal?

-» SOCIAL STUDIES & SCIENCE QUIZ WHIZ «-

Mammals

What is a baby horse called?

-» SOCIAL STUDIES & SCIENCE QUIZ WHIZ «-

Mammals

What term is applied to animals that are active at night?

-» SOCIAL STUDIES & SCIENCE QUIZ WHIZ «-

Mammals

Is a group of lions called a colony, a pride, a skulk, or a gang?

-» SOCIAL STUDIES & SCIENCE QUIZ WHIZ «-

Mammals

What is a male pig called?

→» SOCIAL STUDIES & SCIENCE QUIZ WHIZ «←
Mammals

the elephant

→» SOCIAL STUDIES & SCIENCE QUIZ WHIZ «←
Mammals

vertebrates

→» SOCIAL STUDIES & SCIENCE QUIZ WHIZ «←
Mammals

nocturnal

→» SOCIAL STUDIES & SCIENCE QUIZ WHIZ «←
Mammals

a foal
(colt—male; filly—female)

→» SOCIAL STUDIES & SCIENCE QUIZ WHIZ «←
Mammals

a boar

→» SOCIAL STUDIES & SCIENCE QUIZ WHIZ «←
Mammals

a pride

-» SOCIAL STUDIES & SCIENCE QUIZ WHIZ «-
Mammals

Do most tigers live in Europe, Asia, South America, or Australia?

-» SOCIAL STUDIES & SCIENCE QUIZ WHIZ «-
Mammals

What is a baby zebra called?

-» SOCIAL STUDIES & SCIENCE QUIZ WHIZ «-
Mammals

Is a Saint Bernard a type of lion, dog, cat, or horse?

-» SOCIAL STUDIES & SCIENCE QUIZ WHIZ «-
Mammals

What is the hard covering on the feet of cattle, horses, and deer called?

-» SOCIAL STUDIES & SCIENCE QUIZ WHIZ «-
Mammals

Which of the following is *not* a type of bear: yellow, brown, black, grizzly, or polar?

-» SOCIAL STUDIES & SCIENCE QUIZ WHIZ «-
Mammals

What animal has brownish-gray fur, a pointed face, and black markings that resemble a mask: a raccoon, a beaver, a camel, or a skunk?

-» SOCIAL STUDIES & SCIENCE QUIZ WHIZ «-

Mammals

a colt

-» SOCIAL STUDIES & SCIENCE QUIZ WHIZ «-

Mammals

Asia

-» SOCIAL STUDIES & SCIENCE QUIZ WHIZ «-

Mammals

hoof or hooves

-» SOCIAL STUDIES & SCIENCE QUIZ WHIZ «-

Mammals

dog

-» SOCIAL STUDIES & SCIENCE QUIZ WHIZ «-

Mammals

a raccoon

-» SOCIAL STUDIES & SCIENCE QUIZ WHIZ «-

Mammals

yellow

-» SOCIAL STUDIES & SCIENCE QUIZ WHIZ «-
Mammals

Which of these animals is *not* a kind of ape: a monkey, a gibbon, an orangutan, or a gorilla?

-» SOCIAL STUDIES & SCIENCE QUIZ WHIZ «-
Mammals

Do most giraffes live in Africa, Antarctica, Asia, or South America?

-» SOCIAL STUDIES & SCIENCE QUIZ WHIZ «-
Mammals

Which of the following is *not* a mammal: an okapi, an ibex, a smelt, or a zebu?

-» SOCIAL STUDIES & SCIENCE QUIZ WHIZ «-
Mammals

What is a group of wolves called?

-» SOCIAL STUDIES & SCIENCE QUIZ WHIZ «-
Mammals

Which of the following animals live in the mountains of South America: gazelles, koalas, bison, or alpacas?

-» SOCIAL STUDIES & SCIENCE QUIZ WHIZ «-
Mammals

To which of the following families does a mink belong: cat, weasel, dog, or wolf?

Africa

a monkey

a pack

a smelt (fish)

weasel

alpacas

-»> SOCIAL STUDIES & SCIENCE QUIZ WHIZ «-
Mammals

What is the fastest land animal?

-»> SOCIAL STUDIES & SCIENCE QUIZ WHIZ «-
Mammals

What term is applied to animals that are active during the day?

-»> SOCIAL STUDIES & SCIENCE QUIZ WHIZ «-
Mammals

What are the organs through which mammals obtain oxygen from the air called?

-»> SOCIAL STUDIES & SCIENCE QUIZ WHIZ «-
Mammals

Is a gazelle a type of bear, antelope, monkey, or tiger?

-»> SOCIAL STUDIES & SCIENCE QUIZ WHIZ «-
Mammals

What name is given to gnawing animals such as rats, porcupines, and beavers?

-»> SOCIAL STUDIES & SCIENCE QUIZ WHIZ «-
Mammals

What are animals, such as kangaroos and opossums, that carry their young in a pouch called?

Mammals

diurnal

Mammals

the cheetah

Mammals

antelope

Mammals

lungs

Mammals

marsupials

Mammals

rodents

-»> SOCIAL STUDIES & SCIENCE QUIZ WHIZ «-
Birds, Bugs, & Reptiles

How many legs does an insect have?

-»> SOCIAL STUDIES & SCIENCE QUIZ WHIZ «-
Birds, Bugs, & Reptiles

Which of the following is one of the largest living reptiles: a saltwater crocodile, a caiman, or an alligator?

-»> SOCIAL STUDIES & SCIENCE QUIZ WHIZ «-
Birds, Bugs, & Reptiles

What is another name for an insect's feelers?

-»> SOCIAL STUDIES & SCIENCE QUIZ WHIZ «-
Birds, Bugs, & Reptiles

Which of the following do bees *not* feed on: nectar, milk, or pollen?

-»> SOCIAL STUDIES & SCIENCE QUIZ WHIZ «-
Birds, Bugs, & Reptiles

Which of the following is a large, poisonous snake found in Asia and Africa: rat snake, milk snake, corn snake, or cobra?

-»> SOCIAL STUDIES & SCIENCE QUIZ WHIZ «-
Birds, Bugs, & Reptiles

Is a yellow jacket a type of ant, wasp, beetle, or fly?

-» SOCIAL STUDIES & SCIENCE QUIZ WHIZ «-

Birds, Bugs, & Reptiles

the saltwater crocodile

-» SOCIAL STUDIES & SCIENCE QUIZ WHIZ «-

Birds, Bugs, & Reptiles

six legs

-» SOCIAL STUDIES & SCIENCE QUIZ WHIZ «-

Birds, Bugs, & Reptiles

milk

-» SOCIAL STUDIES & SCIENCE QUIZ WHIZ «-

Birds, Bugs, & Reptiles

antennae

-» SOCIAL STUDIES & SCIENCE QUIZ WHIZ «-

Birds, Bugs, & Reptiles

wasp

-» SOCIAL STUDIES & SCIENCE QUIZ WHIZ «-

Birds, Bugs, & Reptiles

cobra

-» SOCIAL STUDIES & SCIENCE QUIZ WHIZ «-
Birds, Bugs, & Reptiles

The body of an insect consists of how many segments?

-» SOCIAL STUDIES & SCIENCE QUIZ WHIZ «-
Birds, Bugs, & Reptiles

Which is *not* a bird: a robin, a penguin, a chicken, or a gerbil?

-» SOCIAL STUDIES & SCIENCE QUIZ WHIZ «-
Birds, Bugs, & Reptiles

On which part of an insect's body are the antennae located?

-» SOCIAL STUDIES & SCIENCE QUIZ WHIZ «-
Birds, Bugs, & Reptiles

What is a snake's body covered with: hair, fur, scales, or feathers?

-» SOCIAL STUDIES & SCIENCE QUIZ WHIZ «-
Birds, Bugs, & Reptiles

What do you call a group of bees?

-» SOCIAL STUDIES & SCIENCE QUIZ WHIZ «-
Birds, Bugs, & Reptiles

What part of a turtle's body provides protection for the reptile?

-» SOCIAL STUDIES & SCIENCE QUIZ WHIZ «-

Birds, Bugs, & Reptiles

a gerbil

-» SOCIAL STUDIES & SCIENCE QUIZ WHIZ «-

Birds, Bugs, & Reptiles

three segments

-» SOCIAL STUDIES & SCIENCE QUIZ WHIZ «-

Birds, Bugs, & Reptiles

scales

-» SOCIAL STUDIES & SCIENCE QUIZ WHIZ «-

Birds, Bugs, & Reptiles

the head or the first part

-» SOCIAL STUDIES & SCIENCE QUIZ WHIZ «-

Birds, Bugs, & Reptiles

its shell

-» SOCIAL STUDIES & SCIENCE QUIZ WHIZ «-

Birds, Bugs, & Reptiles

a swarm or hive

•» SOCIAL STUDIES & SCIENCE QUIZ WHIZ «•

Birds, Bugs, & Reptiles

Which of the following is *not* a snake: gavial, anaconda, cobra, cottonmouth?

•» SOCIAL STUDIES & SCIENCE QUIZ WHIZ «•

Birds, Bugs, & Reptiles

What term is given to the process of a caterpillar becoming a butterfly and a tadpole becoming a frog?

•» SOCIAL STUDIES & SCIENCE QUIZ WHIZ «•

Birds, Bugs, & Reptiles

What is the national bird of the United States?

•» SOCIAL STUDIES & SCIENCE QUIZ WHIZ «•

Birds, Bugs, & Reptiles

Although they are similar, which reptile has the shorter, wider head: an alligator or a crocodile?

•» SOCIAL STUDIES & SCIENCE QUIZ WHIZ «•

Birds, Bugs, & Reptiles

What is the larva of a butterfly or moth called?

•» SOCIAL STUDIES & SCIENCE QUIZ WHIZ «•

Birds, Bugs, & Reptiles

Which bird does *not* have a sharp, hooked beak: a finch, an eagle, or a hawk?

Birds, Bugs, & Reptiles

metamorphosis

Birds, Bugs, & Reptiles

gavial

Birds, Bugs, & Reptiles

an alligator

Birds, Bugs, & Reptiles

the bald eagle

Birds, Bugs, & Reptiles

a finch

Birds, Bugs, & Reptiles

a caterpillar

-»> SOCIAL STUDIES & SCIENCE QUIZ WHIZ «<-

Birds, Bugs, & Reptiles

Which is *not* a stage of metamorphosis: egg, larvae, hive, or pupa?

-»> SOCIAL STUDIES & SCIENCE QUIZ WHIZ «<-

Birds, Bugs, & Reptiles

What is the name of the large groups in which ants live?

-»> SOCIAL STUDIES & SCIENCE QUIZ WHIZ «<-

Birds, Bugs, & Reptiles

What is the part of an insect's body that is between the head and the abdomen?

-»> SOCIAL STUDIES & SCIENCE QUIZ WHIZ «<-

Birds, Bugs, & Reptiles

What does a reptile do when it molts?

-»> SOCIAL STUDIES & SCIENCE QUIZ WHIZ «<-

Birds, Bugs, & Reptiles

Which bird can fly backward?

-»> SOCIAL STUDIES & SCIENCE QUIZ WHIZ «<-

Birds, Bugs, & Reptiles

Which of the following is *not* an insect: a beetle, a spider, a wasp, or a dragonfly?

colonies

hive

sheds its skin

the thorax

a spider

the hummingbird

➤» SOCIAL STUDIES & SCIENCE QUIZ WHIZ «◄
Birds, Bugs, & Reptiles

Which of these snakes does not kill its prey by constriction: a boa, a rattlesnake, a python, or an anaconda?

➤» SOCIAL STUDIES & SCIENCE QUIZ WHIZ «◄
Birds, Bugs, & Reptiles

Which is *not* a characteristic of a bird: it's cold-blooded, it lays eggs, it has a backbone, or it has wings?

➤» SOCIAL STUDIES & SCIENCE QUIZ WHIZ «◄
Birds, Bugs, & Reptiles

What is the name of the bird that is pink, has a long neck and legs, and has webbed feet?

➤» SOCIAL STUDIES & SCIENCE QUIZ WHIZ «◄
Birds, Bugs, & Reptiles

How many pairs of wings do butterflies have?

➤» SOCIAL STUDIES & SCIENCE QUIZ WHIZ «◄
Birds, Bugs, & Reptiles

What kind of reptile is a Gila monster: a snake, a turtle, a crocodile, or a lizard?

➤» SOCIAL STUDIES & SCIENCE QUIZ WHIZ «◄
Birds, Bugs, & Reptiles

Which of the following is *not* a lizard: gecko, python, moloch, or chameleon?

-» SOCIAL STUDIES & SCIENCE QUIZ WHIZ «-

Birds, Bugs, & Reptiles

it's cold-blooded

-» SOCIAL STUDIES & SCIENCE QUIZ WHIZ «-

Birds, Bugs, & Reptiles

a rattlesnake

-» SOCIAL STUDIES & SCIENCE QUIZ WHIZ «-

Birds, Bugs, & Reptiles

two pairs

-» SOCIAL STUDIES & SCIENCE QUIZ WHIZ «-

Birds, Bugs, & Reptiles

a flamingo

-» SOCIAL STUDIES & SCIENCE QUIZ WHIZ «-

Birds, Bugs, & Reptiles

python

-» SOCIAL STUDIES & SCIENCE QUIZ WHIZ «-

Birds, Bugs, & Reptiles

a lizard

-» SOCIAL STUDIES & SCIENCE QUIZ WHIZ «-
Birds, Bugs, & Reptiles

Which of the following is *not* a reptile: lizard, alligator, salamander, or snake?

-» SOCIAL STUDIES & SCIENCE QUIZ WHIZ «-
Birds, Bugs, & Reptiles

Is a *talon* a type of beak, eye, claw, or tail of a bird of prey such as a hawk?

-» SOCIAL STUDIES & SCIENCE QUIZ WHIZ «-
Birds, Bugs, & Reptiles

Reptiles breathe by means of which organ?

-» SOCIAL STUDIES & SCIENCE QUIZ WHIZ «-
Birds, Bugs, & Reptiles

Which is *not* a color found on a coral snake: green, red, black or yellow?

-» SOCIAL STUDIES & SCIENCE QUIZ WHIZ «-
Birds, Bugs, & Reptiles

Which of the following birds is the only one that can fly: a penguin, an oriole, an emu, or an ostrich?

-» SOCIAL STUDIES & SCIENCE QUIZ WHIZ «-
Birds, Bugs, & Reptiles

Which of the following birds has webbed feet: a cardinal, a sparrow, a pelican, or a toucan?

-»> SOCIAL STUDIES & SCIENCE QUIZ WHIZ «<-
Birds, Bugs, & Reptiles

a claw

-»> SOCIAL STUDIES & SCIENCE QUIZ WHIZ «<-
Birds, Bugs, & Reptiles

salamander

-»> SOCIAL STUDIES & SCIENCE QUIZ WHIZ «<-
Birds, Bugs, & Reptiles

green

-»> SOCIAL STUDIES & SCIENCE QUIZ WHIZ «<-
Birds, Bugs, & Reptiles

lungs

-»> SOCIAL STUDIES & SCIENCE QUIZ WHIZ «<-
Birds, Bugs, & Reptiles

a pelican

-»> SOCIAL STUDIES & SCIENCE QUIZ WHIZ «<-
Birds, Bugs, & Reptiles

an oriole

-» SOCIAL STUDIES & SCIENCE QUIZ WHIZ «-

The Human Body

What organ pumps blood to all parts of the human body?

-» SOCIAL STUDIES & SCIENCE QUIZ WHIZ «-

The Human Body

Which curved bones in the chest protect the heart and lungs?

-» SOCIAL STUDIES & SCIENCE QUIZ WHIZ «-

The Human Body

Which part of the human body is the center of learning, thought, memory, and emotions?

-» SOCIAL STUDIES & SCIENCE QUIZ WHIZ «-

The Human Body

What is the black part of your eye called?

-» SOCIAL STUDIES & SCIENCE QUIZ WHIZ «-

The Human Body

What are the two organs for breathing that are found in the chest of humans called?

-» SOCIAL STUDIES & SCIENCE QUIZ WHIZ «-

The Human Body

What is the name of the long tube that extends down from the stomach and carries and digests food and stores waste products?

the ribs

the heart

the pupil

the brain

the intestine

lungs

The Human Body

Is the colon the main part of the large intestine, the heart, the lungs, or the liver?

The Human Body

What is a hole in a tooth that is caused by decay called?

The Human Body

Is the sense by which the flavor of something in the mouth is noticed called smell, sight, feel, or taste?

The Human Body

What are the two outer openings of the nose where air is taken in and let out called?

The Human Body

Is the colored part of the eye called the cornea, the pupil, the iris, or the lens?

The Human Body

What is the outer covering of the human body called?

a cavity

the large intestine

nostrils

taste

skin

the iris

The Human Body

Are the sharp, front teeth used for cutting and biting called molars, bicuspids, incisors, or cuspids?

The Human Body

What are the blood vessels that carry oxygen-rich blood away from the heart called: aortas, arteries, lungs, veins?

The Human Body

Is the "funny bone" found in the wrist, fingers, knee, or elbow?

The Human Body

How many chambers make up the human heart?

The Human Body

What is the name of the moisture that is given off through the pores of the skin?

The Human Body

How many permanent teeth do most adults have: 25, 32, 36, or 40?

SOCIAL STUDIES & SCIENCE QUIZ WHIZ
The Human Body

arteries

SOCIAL STUDIES & SCIENCE QUIZ WHIZ
The Human Body

incisors

SOCIAL STUDIES & SCIENCE QUIZ WHIZ
The Human Body

four chambers

SOCIAL STUDIES & SCIENCE QUIZ WHIZ
The Human Body

elbow

SOCIAL STUDIES & SCIENCE QUIZ WHIZ
The Human Body

32 teeth

SOCIAL STUDIES & SCIENCE QUIZ WHIZ
The Human Body

perspiration or sweat

The Human Body

Is the upper part of a tooth that can be seen above the gum called the iris, the crown, the root, or the pulp?

The Human Body

Are the smallest bones in the human body located in the spine, the ear, the thigh, or the arm?

The Human Body

Is each of the upper chambers of the heart called a ventricle, an atrium, a valve, or an artery?

The Human Body

What is the place where one bone connects to another called: a tendon, an artery, a joint, or a muscle?

The Human Body

Is the tibia a bone found in the lower leg, arm, spine, or skull?

The Human Body

How many bones make up the adult human body: 106, 150, 206, 250?

the ear

the crown

a joint

an atrium

206 bones

lower leg

The Human Body

What is the name of the soft tissue, found inside bones, that makes blood cells?

The Human Body

Is the femur a bone found in the skull, arm, leg, or pelvis?

The Human Body

The *patella* is another name for what bone in the body?

The Human Body

What is the name of the tough tissue that connects muscles to bones?

The Human Body

What is the chemical breakdown of food in the body called?

The Human Body

What are the bundles of fibers that carry messages between the brain and spinal cord and other parts of the body called?

The Human Body

leg

The Human Body

marrow

The Human Body

tendon

The Human Body

the kneecap

The Human Body

nerves

The Human Body

digestion

What is the hardest substance in the human body?

Which organ in the body makes bile, cleans the blood, and stores fats and sugars?

What are the blood vessels that carry blood to the heart called?

What is the thin tissue, stretched like the top of a drum, inside the ear called?

Is the *trachea* another name for the kneecap, the windpipe, the spine, or the shoulder?

What is the gland near the stomach that makes digestive juices and hormones such as insulin called?

-» **SOCIAL STUDIES & SCIENCE QUIZ WHIZ** «-
The Human Body

the liver

-» **SOCIAL STUDIES & SCIENCE QUIZ WHIZ** «-
The Human Body

tooth enamel

-» **SOCIAL STUDIES & SCIENCE QUIZ WHIZ** «-
The Human Body

the eardrum

-» **SOCIAL STUDIES & SCIENCE QUIZ WHIZ** «-
The Human Body

veins

-» **SOCIAL STUDIES & SCIENCE QUIZ WHIZ** «-
The Human Body

the pancreas

-» **SOCIAL STUDIES & SCIENCE QUIZ WHIZ** «-
The Human Body

windpipe

⬤≫ SOCIAL STUDIES & SCIENCE QUIZ WHIZ ≪⬤
Science Grab Bag

Is a storm with very strong winds and heavy rains called a mist, a hurricane, an icicle, or a warm front?

⬤≫ SOCIAL STUDIES & SCIENCE QUIZ WHIZ ≪⬤
Science Grab Bag

Which star is the source of the earth's light and heat?

⬤≫ SOCIAL STUDIES & SCIENCE QUIZ WHIZ ≪⬤
Science Grab Bag

Which planet is known as the "red planet"?

⬤≫ SOCIAL STUDIES & SCIENCE QUIZ WHIZ ≪⬤
Science Grab Bag

In which direction does the sun rise: north, south, east, or west?

⬤≫ SOCIAL STUDIES & SCIENCE QUIZ WHIZ ≪⬤
Science Grab Bag

How long does it take for the earth to complete one orbit around the sun?

⬤≫ SOCIAL STUDIES & SCIENCE QUIZ WHIZ ≪⬤
Science Grab Bag

In which galaxy is the planet Earth?

Science Grab Bag

the sun

Science Grab Bag

a hurricane

Science Grab Bag

east

Science Grab Bag

Mars

Science Grab Bag

the Milky Way galaxy

Science Grab Bag

365 days or one year

→» SOCIAL STUDIES & SCIENCE QUIZ WHIZ «←
Science Grab Bag

What is the earth's only natural satellite that revolves from east to west once every 29½ days?

→» SOCIAL STUDIES & SCIENCE QUIZ WHIZ «←
Science Grab Bag

Which word does *not* belong: Libra, Mars, Saturn, or Neptune?

→» SOCIAL STUDIES & SCIENCE QUIZ WHIZ «←
Science Grab Bag

How many planets are in our solar system?

→» SOCIAL STUDIES & SCIENCE QUIZ WHIZ «←
Science Grab Bag

Is frozen rain called haze, sleet, dew, or fog?

→» SOCIAL STUDIES & SCIENCE QUIZ WHIZ «←
Science Grab Bag

What is a powerful storm with dark, funnel-shaped clouds called?

→» SOCIAL STUDIES & SCIENCE QUIZ WHIZ «←
Science Grab Bag

What is a flash of light caused by electricity moving between clouds called?

Libra (not the name of a planet)

the moon

sleet

nine planets

lightning

a tornado

·» SOCIAL STUDIES & SCIENCE QUIZ WHIZ «·
Science Grab Bag

What is a unit for measuring the force of an electric current called?

·» SOCIAL STUDIES & SCIENCE QUIZ WHIZ «·
Science Grab Bag

What is a bright object in space that looks like a star with a long tail of light called?

·» SOCIAL STUDIES & SCIENCE QUIZ WHIZ «·
Science Grab Bag

What is the chemical symbol for water?

·» SOCIAL STUDIES & SCIENCE QUIZ WHIZ «·
Science Grab Bag

Which planet is the smallest in our solar system?

·» SOCIAL STUDIES & SCIENCE QUIZ WHIZ «·
Science Grab Bag

What is a natural or man-made body that revolves around a planet called?

·» SOCIAL STUDIES & SCIENCE QUIZ WHIZ «·
Science Grab Bag

What is the science that deals with the sun, stars, moon, planets, and other heavenly bodies called?

-» SOCIAL STUDIES & SCIENCE QUIZ WHIZ «-

Science Grab Bag

a comet

-» SOCIAL STUDIES & SCIENCE QUIZ WHIZ «-

Science Grab Bag

a volt

-» SOCIAL STUDIES & SCIENCE QUIZ WHIZ «-

Science Grab Bag

Pluto

-» SOCIAL STUDIES & SCIENCE QUIZ WHIZ «-

Science Grab Bag

H_2O

-» SOCIAL STUDIES & SCIENCE QUIZ WHIZ «-

Science Grab Bag

astronomy

-» SOCIAL STUDIES & SCIENCE QUIZ WHIZ «-

Science Grab Bag

a satellite

Science Grab Bag

Is a bar or rod used to lift things or to pry things open called a levy, a level, a crane, or a lever?

Science Grab Bag

Which planet is the largest in our solar system and the fifth closest planet to the sun?

Science Grab Bag

Is *cumulus* a kind of flower, machine, cloud, or mineral?

Science Grab Bag

Which is the fourth largest planet and the eighth planet in order of distance from the sun: Earth, Venus, Uranus, or Neptune?

Science Grab Bag

Which word does *not* belong: catapult, flint, pump, or crane?

Science Grab Bag

Which planet is the second smallest and the one closest to the sun?

-» **SOCIAL STUDIES & SCIENCE QUIZ WHIZ** «-
Science Grab Bag

Jupiter

-» **SOCIAL STUDIES & SCIENCE QUIZ WHIZ** «-
Science Grab Bag

a lever

-» **SOCIAL STUDIES & SCIENCE QUIZ WHIZ** «-
Science Grab Bag

Neptune

-» **SOCIAL STUDIES & SCIENCE QUIZ WHIZ** «-
Science Grab Bag

cloud

-» **SOCIAL STUDIES & SCIENCE QUIZ WHIZ** «-
Science Grab Bag

Mercury

-» **SOCIAL STUDIES & SCIENCE QUIZ WHIZ** «-
Science Grab Bag

flint (not a type of machine)

➤➤ SOCIAL STUDIES & SCIENCE QUIZ WHIZ ◄◄
Science Grab Bag

What is the smallest particle of a chemical element that has all the properties of that element called?

➤➤ SOCIAL STUDIES & SCIENCE QUIZ WHIZ ◄◄
Science Grab Bag

What is a grooved wheel that a rope can be pulled over called?

➤➤ SOCIAL STUDIES & SCIENCE QUIZ WHIZ ◄◄
Science Grab Bag

Which planet is the one nearest Earth and the second planet in order of distance from the sun?

➤➤ SOCIAL STUDIES & SCIENCE QUIZ WHIZ ◄◄
Science Grab Bag

Which of the following is *not* part of a comet: ice, electricity, dust particles, or frozen gases?

➤➤ SOCIAL STUDIES & SCIENCE QUIZ WHIZ ◄◄
Science Grab Bag

Which is *not* a form of precipitation: sleet, hail, rain, clouds, or snow?

➤➤ SOCIAL STUDIES & SCIENCE QUIZ WHIZ ◄◄
Science Grab Bag

Which two planets have no known moons: Pluto and Saturn, Mercury and Venus, or Uranus and Mars?

->> SOCIAL STUDIES & SCIENCE QUIZ WHIZ <<-

Science Grab Bag

a pulley

->> SOCIAL STUDIES & SCIENCE QUIZ WHIZ <<-

Science Grab Bag

an atom

->> SOCIAL STUDIES & SCIENCE QUIZ WHIZ <<-

Science Grab Bag

electricity

->> SOCIAL STUDIES & SCIENCE QUIZ WHIZ <<-

Science Grab Bag

Venus

->> SOCIAL STUDIES & SCIENCE QUIZ WHIZ <<-

Science Grab Bag

Mercury and Venus

->> SOCIAL STUDIES & SCIENCE QUIZ WHIZ <<-

Science Grab Bag

clouds

SOCIAL STUDIES & SCIENCE QUIZ WHIZ
Science Grab Bag

What is the center of an atom called?

SOCIAL STUDIES & SCIENCE QUIZ WHIZ
Science Grab Bag

What is a tiny particle that moves around the nucleus of an atom and has a negative electrical charge called?

SOCIAL STUDIES & SCIENCE QUIZ WHIZ
Science Grab Bag

What name is given to a gigantic tropical storm that occurs in the western Pacific Ocean?

SOCIAL STUDIES & SCIENCE QUIZ WHIZ
Science Grab Bag

Which planet is usually farthest from the sun?

SOCIAL STUDIES & SCIENCE QUIZ WHIZ
Science Grab Bag

At what temperature does water freeze?

SOCIAL STUDIES & SCIENCE QUIZ WHIZ
Science Grab Bag

What are the three states of matter?

-» SOCIAL STUDIES & SCIENCE QUIZ WHIZ «-
Science Grab Bag

an electron

-» SOCIAL STUDIES & SCIENCE QUIZ WHIZ «-
Science Grab Bag

the nucleus

-» SOCIAL STUDIES & SCIENCE QUIZ WHIZ «-
Science Grab Bag

Pluto

-» SOCIAL STUDIES & SCIENCE QUIZ WHIZ «-
Science Grab Bag

a typhoon

-» SOCIAL STUDIES & SCIENCE QUIZ WHIZ «-
Science Grab Bag

solid, liquid, and gas

-» SOCIAL STUDIES & SCIENCE QUIZ WHIZ «-
Science Grab Bag

0° C or 32° F